October 16, 2021

D0769753

Own Your Day

How Sales Leaders Master
Time Management,
Minimize Distractions, and
Create Their Ideal Lives

Keith Rosen

Own Your Day: How Sales Leaders Master Time Management, Minimize Distractions, and Create Their Ideal Lives by Keith Rosen

Editor: Keith Nerdin
Cover Design: Keith Nerdin
Interior Design: Keith Nerdin

Published by Ember Publishing. EMBER and associated logos are trademarks and/or registered trademarks of Ember Publishing.

Printed in the United States of America
ISBN 978-0-9863814-3-0

[ABOUT THE AUTHOR]

Keith Rosen

Keith Rosen, a global authority on sales and leadership, is fanatical about your success. Over the past three decades, he has delivered his courses to hundreds of thousands of salespeople and managers in practically every industry, on five continents, and in more than fifty countries.

Keith is the CEO of Profit Builders, named one of the Best Sales Training and Coaching Companies worldwide. He has written several best-selling books. His globally acclaimed book *Coaching Salespeople into Sales Champions* won five International Best Book Awards and is the number one best-selling sales-management coaching book.

As a leader in the coaching profession and a pioneer in the field of management coach training, Keith was inducted into the inaugural group of the Top Sales Hall of Fame in recognition of his outstanding contributions in sales and leadership development.

Inc. magazine and *Fast Company* named Keith one of the five most influential executive coaches. He's been featured in *Entrepreneur*, *Inc.*, *Fortune*, the *New York Times*, and the *Wall Street Journal*. He was also featured on the award-winning television show *Mad Men* and was one of the first of only a handful of coaches who earned the distinguished Master Certified Coach designation through the International Coach Federation.

To get Keith's e-books, articles, and videos, visit http://keithrosen.com

[CONTENTS]

[PART ONE—Your Personal Navigation System]

[PART TWO—How to Own Your Day]

[PART THREE—Live Responsibly]

EXTREME MYTH BUSTING

SELF-ACCOUNTABILITY

[PREFACE]

Is Time Management Sexy? Now It Is!

Joe Connolly and I had spoken over the phone only twice before meeting each other in person. Joe worked for the *Wall Street Journal* and had invited me to sit on a panel of experts for a small-business breakfast in New York City. I accepted the invitation, and as we took our positions at the panelists' table, Joe introduced us one by one. Following my introduction, he added, "After speaking with Keith, I knew he was the real deal, especially when I asked him if he could commit to the date. Instead of saying yes on the spot, which, according to Keith can mean you're a 'yesaholic,' he responded with, 'Thanks, Joe. Let me check my schedule, and I'll get back to you by the end of the day.' So not only is he an expert on time management, he's a guy who practices what he preaches."

The discussion began, and a question came my way: "Hi, Keith," the gentleman began. "What strategies would you suggest to better manage my time?"

I shot back, "Stop trying to manage something you cannot manage in the first place."

Blank stares from the audience. "Let me explain," I said. "But first, let me ask everyone sitting here a question: How many of you are familiar with the expression 'time is money'?"

Almost everyone raised his or her hand.

Then I asked, "By a show of hands, how many of you manage your money in some way? Whether you use a stockbroker, financial advisor, accountant, bank, hidden safe, or just do it yourself? Raise your hand if you manage your money in some way."

Several hundred people raised their hands almost immediately—a good 90 percent of the audience.

Then I asked, "How many of you manage your time as diligently as you manage your money? In other words, raise your hand if you have a consistent, weekly routine you follow from the time you wake up in the morning until the time you end your day. A routine that contains the specific, measurable activities and tasks you engage in that move you closer to your business and career goals, while honoring your priorities and keeping your personal life in harmony."

Not a single hand went up. In a room filled with highly successful professionals, not one person could confidently raise his or her hand and say, "Yes! I have that!" These people were still successful in spite of the fact that they all in some way had just admitted, "I do not treat time like my money. I can benefit from changing how I manage my time and think about my schedule. I do not own my day."

"Isn't that ironic?" I continued. "Here we are, on the surface believing that time is money, yet we're not managing our time and ourselves the way we manage our money. We don't give our time and money the same respect, diligence, and planning.

"And the kicker is, once you choose to invest or spend your time, you don't get it back. You can't double it, invest it, or save it for a rainy day. But you can learn how to do things more efficiently and effectively and create more time to focus on your priorities and what you really want to be doing. That's why it's important to shift the focus from trying to *manage your time* to managing what you can control, which is yourself, your thinking, and the actions you take each day.

"The foundation to living your potential is to first upgrade your relationship with time so that it becomes your ally, not your adversary. Then you can begin the process of developing a routine that can allow you to create and live your ideal life."

Time Management for Sales Managers

I wrote one of my first books, *Time Management for Sales Professionals*, back in 1996. Since then, I've had the privilege of working with sales leaders and their salespeople all over the world.

The one central theme everyone seems to struggle with most is managing their time. Between handling all of their personal and professional responsibilities, it becomes almost impossible to find time to also create a rich and fulfilling life without sacrificing something.

Repeatedly I'd hear the same thing from sales managers: "Keith, I'm bought into coaching. I see the importance of it and understand why it needs to be a priority for my sales team and me. But with all the demands placed on us, it's impossible to find the time to coach people on a consistent basis."

I get it. Most of these sales leaders take their work very seriously and are doing, or trying to do, a great job with the resources available to them. And the majority of them are hitting their business objectives and sales quotas. So one could argue that their current system *works*. Another possibility is, most managers I know are wired to be *survivors!* That means they do what it takes to get the job done, which isn't necessarily a healthy, sustainable strategy. If I were to drop practically any manager on a deserted island, he or she would probably adapt and survive. Just like you survive whenever you're dropped into any new situation. It's in your DNA. You're a warrior—you have a winner's mentality. Never, ever give up. Your competitive nature fuels you to succeed!

It's when you combine that competitive nature with formal training on how to best manage your time, goals, responsibilities, and ultimately your day that you'll experience exponentially higher levels of success, as well as overall harmony and significance in what you do and who you are.

It's just like hiring a new salesperson who has never been trained to sell before. What would you do to ensure their success? You'd put them through training. Why? So that you can make certain that they possess the essential foundation, mind-set, and skill set necessary to thrive in their new role.

The art and science of managing your day with mastery and precision is no different than maximizing your income or ensuring the success of a new hire, while minimizing costly errors from a mishire or faulty onboarding process.

But you already know this.

So let's get started. *10/16/2021*

[ACKNOWLEDGMENTS]

I'm forever fortunate to make the time to enjoy that which is most precious in my life, especially my family. Life is too short to live in regret.

My wife and children will always be my greatest teachers and the center of my world. You continually remind me of what my true priorities are: to be present, to recognize the perfection in every moment, and to appreciate deeply the greatest gift of all—the value of time.

[PART ONE]

Your Personal Navigation System

CHAPTER 1

What's Your Drive to Thrive?

The Foundation of Your Routine

Years ago, when I first began coaching, I was searching for a way to coach people around setting and achieving their goals in a way that was more holistic and effective than what was traditionally being done.

For most people, the greatest challenge wasn't the act of setting their goals. Don't get me wrong. If you were to stop ten people on the street, maybe one would admit that he or she has taken the time to map out goals in written form. What posed the greatest threat to achieving their goals was how they were navigating their day and attempting to deal with everything being hurled at them along the way.

The work I started all those years ago has continued to evolve to this day. And although I'm writing this book for sales leaders focusing on time management, the concepts and ideas in this book apply globally, regardless of your role. Regardless, it's crucial to note that you will get the most value out of this book if you first take some time to clarify and define your:

1. Personal and Professional Vision (Chapter 2)
2. Core Values and Priorities (Chapter 3)
3. Specific and Measurable Goals (Chapter 4)
4. Strategy to Attain Goals (Chapter 5)

Just like building a new home, your vision, goals, and strategy will act as a blueprint for your success. But it's not just about you being able to achieve your goals or generate the results you really want. This is your opportunity to redesign your day, your lifestyle, and ultimately your life so you can begin achieving the levels of peace and harmony you want in life now, rather than later.

So imagine you've been given a blank canvass. This canvass serves one purpose—for you to design, with visually creative and detailed clarity, your ideal life. What masterpiece do you want to create called "_____'s (fill in your name) Awesome Life"? How would it look different than it does today? What are some of the parts of your life today that are already part of your masterpiece? If you're reading this book, then chances are, you're already a successful person in many ways.

What will you do with your time every day? What choices will you make? How will you respond to situations on a daily basis that will ultimately create what you want most in life?

Clarifying the end result in your mind before beginning this process of upgrading and redesigning your day will help you get where you want to go much faster.

After all, it's so much easier to reach your destination when you know where you're going, you know what it looks like, and you have a path to get there.

Why Goals Fail

As I thought about the clients and managers who have struggled the most to reach their goals over the years, I identified these most common reasons that caused them to fail at attaining their goals:

- Overcommitting (too many goals)
- Wrong goal ("should"-based goal, need-driven goal)
- Wrong time
- Wrong strategy
- Wrong resources
- Wrong activities
- Wrong skill
- Unrealistic goals (set up for failure)
- Wrong timeline to complete
- Not aligned with values, lifestyle, or priorities
- Wrong people
- Wrong manager
- Wrong expectations being set or agreed to

If it's ever been a struggle for you to reach bigger goals, keep your resolutions, manage your schedule, or maintain your focus and motivation, then I encourage you to take time to develop your Personal Navigation System. Doing so will enable you to map out a new path to achieve your goals, accelerate your productivity, and generate greater results.

A Personal Navigation System is similar to the navigation system in your car or a mapping app on your phone. It's the system you use to navigate through your career and life. A system that encompasses your vision, priorities, goals, strategy, activities, and routine. A system that provides you with a clear sense of purpose, harmony, passion, and direction.

Running your business or managing your career without having the right goals and Personal Navigation System in place would be equivalent to driving from New York to California without a road map—while wearing a blindfold. You'd wind up somewhere, but it wouldn't be where you originally intended to go.

Road Trip!

When you think about your goals, consider what's needed to achieve them with the least amount of risk and in the least amount of time. You will need the following:

1. A clear destination or vision of what the desired outcome will look like
2. Resources needed

3. A target date of reaching your destination

4. The most effective strategy and resources for arriving at your goal

5. Milestones to achieve along the way

6. Measurable daily activities

Throughout each chapter in part one of this book, I'll refer back to a recent experience I had coaching Chris, the VP of Global Sales at one of the largest IT companies in the world, as he designed his own Personal Navigation System.

Previously, Chris and I had discussed what would soon be a life-altering decision—whether or not to leave his position after eighteen years with the company, a high six-figure salary with benefits, and stock options and instead, venture out on his own and start a brand-new consulting firm.

After weighing his options carefully, and several months deliberating over his decision by mapping out his Personal Navigation System, he made up his mind. After a successful eighteen-year run, Chris was ready to move on. During a coaching session several months before announcing his departure from his role, it was time to get serious. I started our conversation with this question: "If you were to leave your current position and start your own company, what would your goals or intentions be every day? What do you want to create for yourself?"

"Well, I'll tell you what I don't want," he replied. "I don't want to work the hours I'm working now. I don't want to continue traveling down the path I am on. I don't want to miss any more of my kid's games or recitals. I don't want to work for an organization that doesn't put its people first. I don't want my reward for hitting an aggressive quota to be a pat on the back and an even larger quota for the next quarter. I don't want to feel guilty if I don't respond to an e-mail over the weekend. I don't want to travel as much. I don't want to deal with so much office politics. I don't want to be bound by golden handcuffs or have to be forced to work with people I don't like."

The rant continued for another minute or so. I let him continue. He needed to get it out. Then I stated my initial question again.

"Thank you for sharing that, Chris. However, you didn't answer my question."

"What was your question again?"

"My question was, if I recall correctly, when you leave your current position and start your own company, what would be your goals and intentions every day to create what you want for yourself? In other words, describe your ideal life. That includes your career, what you'd be doing every day, with whom, and how that aligns with the priorities in your life."

There was a long pause.

"So are you talking about setting clear goals?"

"That's certainly part of this. Think beyond your goals for a moment. Let's say you achieve them. Then what? What does that look like? How do your goals align with your priorities in your life and the vision of what you want your ideal life and career to look like?"

"My what?"

"Your personal vision."

"C'mon, Keith, you're not getting all spiritual on me now, are you?" Chris responded jokingly.

"Actually, I'm referring to designing your Personal Navigation System. What do you think this means?"

"Like the navigation system in my car?"

"Yes."

"Well, I use that all the time. I just plug in an address and get turn-by-turn directions to wherever I want to go."

"Exactly. Now imagine having that for your life. And just like the navigation system in your car, the first thing you need is a clear destination point."

"My goals, right? I have those."

"Well, that's certainly an endpoint, but there is something that needs to be clarified first that precedes your goals. In fact, without it, you may be setting the wrong goals. Let's call this your personal vision.

"Yet to truly design your ideal life, take ownership of your day, and achieve your goals with the least amount of risk or error, there are some other components that need to be built out for your Personal Navigation System to become effective."

CHAPTER 2

Develop Your Personal and Professional Vision

Your Vision

C an you picture in your mind's eye what your ideal life will look like five years from now? Can you conjure up a vivid picture of how you want your future to look? Are you living your vision today?

To achieve more and attain your goals, it's your responsibility to exercise your *super-vision*. That is, use the ability to see beyond what is happening today to crystallize the picture of what you want your life and career to look like tomorrow.

Why is this such a critical component to mastering your day? Well, if you don't know what you really want and have a clear picture of what that looks like, then how will you know when you get it?

Finally, think about the personal sacrifices you're making in pursuit of your goals and dreams. Are you making the right sacrifices for the right dreams?

A vision is inspiring, compelling, seductive, and exhilarating; something so exciting that it pulls you forward and motivates you to jump out of bed every day with a smile on your face because you know something that most people don't. You know exactly where you are going, why you are heading there, how you're going to get there, and when you will arrive at your desired destination. And most important, you have the utmost confidence that you will.

WHY VISION?

There's a universal law I personally live by: "We attract what we want most."

What if you were able to bring into your life that which is most important to you with the least amount of effort, without having to continually push for it?

Sound appealing? The key here is to be able to pull or attract what you want, rather than push for it. While the principles of attraction have been around for decades, the one part I see missing most is the fact that to attract what you really want, you need to make sure you have the space to do it. Consider for a moment that a closet in your home resembles your life. If it's already jam-packed with other goals, commitments, problems, and things you're putting up with that are dragging you down, then you have no room to attract the good stuff into your life! Clean out your closet of prior commitments and challenges first, and then you'll attract what you want more easily because you've created the space for it to show up—naturally.

When people call me who are interested in working with a coach to achieve bigger, more rewarding goals, one of the first things I say to them or ask them is, "Tell me what the next level of success looks like for you" or "If you were to describe your ideal life/career, what would it look like?"

Interestingly, the responses I typically hear are very similar to what Chris shared with me in the last chapter. That is, I hear what people *don't* want in their lives. These kinds of responses are typically based on prior experiences and situations they've gone through already that they don't want to live through again.

Now, if a person does share what he wants to create in his life, he would typically share very general, vague goals or desires, such as these:

- I want to be more successful.
- I want to make more money.
- I want a better job.
- I want healthier relationships.
- I want a beautiful home.
- I want to get in better physical shape.
- I want to be happy.

As you can see, even if people think they know what they want, it's a far cry from being detailed and specific.

Live with Intention

If you apply the universal law I just mentioned—"We attract what we want most"—then this is what you can expect:

1. If you're vague about what you want, then you'll attract a variety of results, experiences, and people into your life. Life will feel random rather than intentional.

2. If you're focusing on what you don't want, then what you don't want will manifest in your life. Where you direct your energy and thoughts is exactly what you base decisions and actions on. As you can see, this can become a very dangerous and self-sabotaging formula, indeed.

It's not enough to say, "I want to be happier, richer, or healthier." To achieve what you want most, it's critical to clarify what success looks like in every area of your life (career, relationships, well-being, finances, attitude, environment, happiness, etc.) and write it down. Be as specific as possible. How much money do you want to have for retirement? By when? What would you do with it? What does your ideal career/business or ideal personal relationship look like? Envision and write down the activities, experiences, or results that are going to genuinely excite and inspire you on a consistent, daily basis!

We Never Grow Past What We Believe to Be Possible

Although we may have a great vision for ourselves in the future, we often place a self-imposed limitation on our success by saying things such as "but that's not being realistic." We never grow past what we believe to be possible. Expand your peripheral vision by broadening your view of what you think. Find your inner limitation and push through that to create what can be.

Alexander Calder, an American sculptor who originated the mobile, once said, "A great artist is a great artist because they perceive the world as if it were observed for the very first time." Let go of your current perceptions that are inhibiting your ability to achieve more, and begin exploring greater possibilities for yourself. This is what allows casual doodlers to become world-renowned artists and basketball novices to become NBA all-stars.

Take the time to discover what you truly want. What would make this year an incredible year for you? Dream really big! What masterpiece do you want to create?

Keep in mind that some of the things you list in your vision may already be present in your life. If so, congratulate yourself on already achieving some of the things that will create your ideal life! Include the things you have attained, as well as the things you want and need to work toward. You don't want to lose sight of what you have already achieved that remain a priority. If developing a close and meaningful relationship with your spouse is a central part of your vision and this is something you feel you have already nurtured, you want to ensure that it still makes it into your documented vision to keep that relationship strong and vibrant.

Upgrade Your Relationship with Fear

In my book *Coaching Salespeople into Sales Champions*, I first introduced this concept. It's so crucial to creating a powerful vision—which will in turn provide the solid foundation needed to master time management—that I felt compelled to include a mention here as well. Now that your vision is coming into focus, what are you putting in your fuel tank every day to provide you with the momentum and energy needed to engage in the right activities that will move you closer to your vision?

Do you focus your energy, efforts, and goals on what you want to achieve, or are you like Chris and most other people and focus more on what you want to avoid instead?

Although we want to improve our lives and achieve more both personally and professionally, many of our decisions are governed by fear. Sure, we want to prevent unwanted situations from occurring, but the irony is, when we set goals or make decisions hoping to avoid situations we don't want to experience in life, we often make decisions about future events that are not even real! Other times we allow vivid memories of unpleasant past experiences to grab hold, and we try to make sure we never end up in that kind of situation again. (Examples: "Missed quota once, don't want that to happen again." "Got bitten by a dog when I was a kid. Today, I stay away from dogs.")

Granted, the feeling of fear is very real; I'm not disputing that. Fear is a feeling or emotion, like happiness, anger, disappointment, peacefulness, excitement, or sadness. These feelings often trigger a physiological reaction, such as perspiration, tightening of muscles, or an elevated heart rate, which reinforces our belief that fear is also physiologically real.

Two parts that make up the experience of fear. One component is the feeling of fear, and the other is the very thing we actually fear or worry about.

Unfortunately, most people collapse *what* they fear and the *feeling* of fear together without distinguishing between these two parts. As such, we have a tendency to resist fear, perceive it as a threat or weakness, and make it our adversary rather than embracing fear as our greatest teacher.

Here's the typical process. You look at past problems, negative experiences, or failures and assume they will happen again. (Example: "The last time I tried that, it was a disaster. So, why put myself in that situation again?") Consequently, you make decisions with the intention of avoiding what you believe would happen in the worst-case scenario. The real cost here is, you wind up basing your decisions on assumptions ("It will happen again") rather than facts. You're also directing your energy toward avoiding something you don't want to happen instead of focusing your energy and efforts on evaluating your processes and approach so that you can achieve what you really want.

Chris tapped his finger nervously on his desk, sensing I was about to challenge him even further. "Think about the three points in time: the past, the present, and the future," I said. "Now, where do your greatest fears live?"

"I guess what I'm afraid of are all the things that can go wrong," Chris said.

"Exactly!" I proclaimed. "What you fear is the negative expectation or assumption of what you *don't* want to happen in the future and is *never* happening in the present. Even if the future is in two minutes, two days, or two months, it's still the future. The good news is, since that which you fear lives in the future ("I'm not going to make my quota!"), you can defuse the fear and make better decisions by bringing yourself into the present moment. This causes fear to lose its powerful grip on you.

"If we are pushed to avoid consequences or what we don't want to happen, conversely we are pulled toward what we do want: pleasure. Because fear is the negative assumption of the outcome, try shifting your focus to the positive outcome or what you *do* want to create instead of what you're trying to avoid.

"The key point here is, your fears are just as *real* as your dreams! But as long as you give more power to your fears rather than your dreams and goals, your fears will always seem as if they are more of a reality, and in turn, they will get the better of you," I told Chris. "Think about it for a moment. They are both visions and pictures of a future that you have constructed or visualized in your mind's eye. Both your fears and dreams are created using the same tool—your imagination!

"The real danger is, if you're really clear with what you *don't* want and don't focus on what you *do* want, then where do you think you're going to continually direct your thoughts and energy? Your goals and dreams can't even compete!

"Identify and empower your dreams and goals, rather than your fears, so that your dreams become the driving force moving you forward. Once you do, you'll begin making choices based on what you want to create instead of what you want to avoid."

Go Do: Uncover Your Vision

Begin the creative process of designing your vision and the ideal lifestyle you want to create for yourself by writing down the answers to the following questions:

- What do you want to have happen most in your life?
- How would you know that your vision has been realized?
- How many years will it take for your vision to be realized?
- What is your role and responsibility in all of this?
- What materials, information, support, and other resources do you need?
- What is prompting, motivating, or inspiring you to want to work on this vision?
- Who will be affected over the next ten years as you achieve your vision?
- What's the real benefit/payoff to you for working on this vision?
- How does this vision enhance your life? Your family, friends, and community?
- How many hours in a typical workday would you be working?

- What is your desired income, and what is your minimum required income?

- Who are the people you will be working with?

- What type of clients will you be serving?

- What type of products/services will you be offering?

- What will your day be filled with? What activities will you be responsible for?

- What level of autonomy will you have?

- Where will you work? (geographic location, office, home office, travel, and so on)

- What are the fears or limiting thinking that's keeping you from moving forward without hesitation? What is going to prevent you from manifesting this in your life?

- Who do you need to be (or become) to achieve, create, or succeed at this? What assumptions do you need to challenge? What part of your attitude and mind-set needs to change for the better?

- What would achieving this vision mean to you personally and professionally?

10/16/2021

CHAPTER 3

Identify Your Core Values and Priorities

Who You Are Matters Most

When I was on vacation with my family recently in Florida, after two days of back-to-back planned activities, we decided to spend most of the following day relaxing at the beach. It was a beautiful day. Nice and warm but not blistering hot. No humidity, either. The waves were big enough to have fun playing in, but not too big to be dangerous. I leaned back in a lounge chair and absorbed my surroundings. Most people seemed to be just like us—on vacation and appearing to enjoy themselves—except for this one guy. He was probably in his late forties and was occupying a lounge chair about twenty feet away under the protection of a large umbrella. Without blinking, his fingers hammered ruthlessly at the submissive keys on his black laptop. Only phone calls of a distinct ringtone were allowed to disrupt his pounding cadence. I tried focusing on the book I was reading but still managed to overhear phrases such as "That's not in the budget," "I'll be back on Monday," and "I can't access that file."

I'll never know for sure, but he didn't seem to be enjoying himself. Perhaps a bona fide emergency erupted at work that absolutely demanded his attention while he made a noble effort to accompany his family to the beach, despite his work demands. Maybe this was going against every core value he had, yet he was still committed to handle a timely issue. Or just maybe his behavior was the norm for him, a manifestation of his values.

Our values determine our priorities, and for him, maybe his priority was his work. Now, I'm not assigning any judgment to that statement if you are choosing what you really want. What is most important to you? What are your values? What would be the most important personal characteristics you could pull from your vision that you would want to use to describe yourself? Would they be different when you're at work and at home?

Sure, you could make two lists—one for business and one for home, but keep one thing in mind. You're still dealing with the same one person: you! Whether work related or more personal in nature, your values are what describe who you are as a person—the same person who goes to work in the morning, the same person who spends time at home, or maybe you're the person who's on his laptop at vacation. Whatever it is you choose, this isn't your dress rehearsal. You have only one life!

Values Flow from Who You Are, Not What You Do

Values are simply who you are when you are fully self-expressed. When you live a life based on your values, you are honoring not only *what* you treasure most but *who* you are. Ask yourself, "Who do I need to be to achieve my vision?" This goes beyond *what* you need to do and focuses on the *who* part of the equation.

Go Do: Write Down Your Values

Take a moment to look at your vision and write down the characteristics, attributes, standards, boundaries, and traits you need to strengthen or adopt to become more of who you were yesterday. What drives you? Who do you need to be to achieve your goals and ideal life?

Although not an exhaustive list, here are a few values to help give you an idea of what to look for that best reflect who you are when you're at your best: Ambition, artistry, bravery, compassion, dignity, frugality, happiness, independence, justice, kindness, learning, mindfulness, neatness, order, patience, reason, sacrifice, trust, valor, wealth, youthfulness, zeal, being challenged, impacting others, adventurous, love, loyal, cautious, passionate, creativity, connection, physically fit, focus, vulnerability, authenticity.

Values Determine Priorities

Attempting to identify your priorities in life before isolating your core values is a waste of time if you're hoping to take back your day and make your vision a reality. Such an exercise would be akin to playing checkers blindfolded. You could move things around, but you'd never know if you were moving the right pieces to the right place. Eleven of my core values are integrity, adventure, contributing, connection, transparency, authenticity, creativity, love, family, friends, and making an impact. Those core values have shaped my priorities, and consequently my life, in dramatic ways. My top three values are what get me out of bed every day:

1. Connection
2. Creativity
3. Contribution

Every day revolves around these three values in some way. Every goal I set or decision I make is with these three values in mind. When I focus on these three values, I'm then able to identify the priorities related to them. My core value of connection results in my family, wife, and children being at the top of my priority list. My core value of creativity results in the writing I do and the books I publish. And my core value of contribution inspires me to continually make an impact through coaching and training, which surface as other top priorities in my life. I need to ensure that these people, projects, and activities end up becoming a part of my lifestyle or my daily routine so that I'm able to honor those values completely and consistently. You will be able to do the same once you identify your values.

Go Do: Write Down Your Priorities

Now that you have outlined your core values, there is one more step before we move on to mapping out your goals—you need to determine the priorities in your life that you're not willing to sacrifice. This way, you can identify the activities you need to engage in and what you are willing to give up today (maybe even a conscious, short-term sacrifice of certain priorities) in pursuit of a bigger dream tomorrow.

When your goals are aligned with your priorities and natural strengths, you'll maintain your integrity and energy and experience greater peace of mind while traveling on your path to achieving meaningful, long-lasting results. You'll find the process of working toward these goals more enjoyable and fulfilling, without feeling as if you're continually pushing for something to happen. Instead, because of this natural alignment, you'll be pulled toward your goal with less effort.

Once you orient your life around your priorities, you'll find that you will actually have fewer goals you'll feel compelled to attain or be driven and consumed by. If you design your life and career around what is most important to you on a daily basis, you'll avoid becoming attached to always trying to create something better at a future point in time, which can rob you of the quality of your life today.

Based on your core values, what are your top priorities? Some examples include family, fitness, travel, sports, music, and professional development. Here is a list of questions to assess whether or not what you are focusing on is a priority, a nonpriority, or a distraction.

Managers can use these questions to coach people around identifying their own priorities:

1. Why is this a priority? Why is this important?

2. Is this aligned with my goals and values, or is it a "should?" (As I wrote about in *Coaching Salespeople into Sales Champions*, a "should" is either an old goal—something that's not aligned with your values, vision, or priorities—or the excrement of someone else's agenda that you feel you "should" take on!)

3. Is this my priority or someone else's?

4. If this is someone else's priority, did I do a good job coaching up to my boss or setting proper expectations regarding what I can deliver on and by when?

5. If I don't focus on and complete this now, how will this impact me and those around me? What will happen?

6. If I do focus on and complete this, what are the benefits and impact on those around me?

7. If I take on this task or project, what are the things that won't be getting done as a result of reallocating my time?

8. Who is relying on me to do this?

9. Did I create an appropriate timeline to begin and complete this task?

10. Is there someone else I can effectively delegate this to?

CHAPTER 4

Define Your Specific and Measurable Goals

Playing by Your Own Rules

I t's time to create your goals! Soon I will be asking you what goals you want most for yourself, your company, and your team over the next twelve months.

Why twelve months? Because goals with shorter timelines tend to lack the significance and weight of yearlong goals. Conversely, when people I coach insist on setting goals with completion dates beyond twelve months, they often lose momentum along the way. Fortunately, because change is the only constant (the economy, marketplace, competition, people, etc.), anything beyond twelve months can easily be rolled up into your vision.

When you set the right goals, you will likely feel excited, a little nervous, and ready to get them started. Generally, there are three categories your goals will fall into:

1. **Mind-set** (e.g., happiness, peace of mind, being intentional, career fulfillment, stronger relationships, being stress/worry free, being/living in the present, personal satisfaction, harmony)

2. **Measurable** (e.g., help salespeople double their bonuses, exceed sales quota of X, improve forecast accuracy by 30 percent, hire five new salespeople, identify and implement a new selling strategy, make an income of X by this date, achieve a quarterly sales goal, buy a new house by this date)

3. **Skill** (further development and *mastery* of communication, selling, leadership, coaching, and time-management skills; spending more time leveraging analytics, metrics, and scorecards; negotiation; life balance; self-care)

Beware of Shoulds

Now that you have created a vision for yourself and identified your values and priorities, it's time to create the goals you really want—not the ones you *should, could, or might* want.

The best game to play is the one where you make up your own rules. Often, we create goals based heavily on what we feel we *should* do. *Shoulds* tend to be formed from what we were taught growing up or from the constant bombardment of advertisements telling us how we *should* look, buy, do, and feel or how we *should* structure our lives.

Think of the things you really, really want to create for yourself as opposed to something you feel you *have* to or *should* be doing. If you're encountering resistance in reaching some of your goals, chances are it's either something you really don't want to be doing, it's an old goal that may not serve you anymore, or you're operating from someone else's agenda!

You are a distinctly unique individual with your very own set of characteristics, values, strengths, and weaknesses. When trying to maintain motivation to achieve goals that are based on other people's expectations, you're always going to encounter resistance. Ironically, this resistance against achieving your goals will primarily come from yourself because they're not your goals. They don't represent your vision or your true identity.

Now imagine a different scenario in which your goals are in precise alignment with your distinctive priorities, values, and individuality, and all of them are in unwavering alignment with your vision of what you absolutely want most in life.

This is when things really start getting exciting!

Priorities vs. Goals—What's the Difference?

Make sure you understand the distinct difference between goals and priorities. When you align your goals with your priorities, you'll achieve the level of success you've always dreamed of.

With the time pressure we place on ourselves when charting our goals, many people often fall short of attaining their goals. Sure, there are many reasons why we may not reach our goals, but before we point our finger or leverage excuses, such as lack of execution, resources, skills, or effective time management, we need to first look at the source of the problem—that is, the goal itself. In other words, are you sure you're setting the right goals?

Here is the differentiation between priorities and goals:

- **Priority**—What is so important and meaningful in your life today (activities, beliefs, lifestyle, principles, standards, hobbies, integrity) that you are not willing to compromise or sacrifice in pursuit of something else (such as a goal)
- **Goal**—A future-based expectation, possibility, measurable end-result, or experience you are working toward creating, achieving or bringing to fruition that has not yet been realized

Priorities are *present focused*, or what is happening. Goals are *future focused*, or what will happen.

Case Study: John's Misaligned Priorities and Goals

John had a goal of being a top producer in his company. As such, he looked at the other top producers and the activities they engaged in that made them successful. The top salespeople were working twelve-hour days, sometimes even seven days a week. Thinking, "It worked for them, so I guess I should do that too," he decided to give up a chunk of his family/personal time and other enjoyable activities/hobbies in his quest to become financially successful.

Although John's priority was spending time with his family, he didn't understand why he felt miserable and encountered resistance while attempting to achieve this goal.

Once he created a personal strategy and a routine for achieving his own bigger goals that supported his lifestyle and priorities without having to sacrifice what mattered most to him, he was able to reach his goals with less effort and enjoyed the process even more.

If you are encountering resistance while attempting to reach certain goals or performing certain tasks, chances are, it's something you really don't want to be doing, it's an old goal that may not serve you anymore (a "should"), or you are operating from someone else's agenda (also a "should")! The bottom line is, these goals don't support your priorities, and you'll continue to feel "off" or out of alignment throughout your pursuit of these misaligned goals.

Take the time to align your goals with your priorities. Otherwise, you'll feel confined or powerless to make changes and will allow situations, circumstances, or other people to influence or control you. Discover what *you* truly want by aligning your goals with the priorities in your life rather than the *shoulds*.

The fact is, *should*-based goals do not support your priorities or personal vision. So if you are unsure whether the goal, activity, or task classifies as a *should*, take a look at your lifestyle, values, and priorities and see if they are all in alignment. If the goal doesn't support them, it's a *should*. Don't *should* on yourself!

Goals Must Be Specific, Measurable and Have a Deadline

My friend, Eric, recently asked if I could review a year-end document of his that included details of his upcoming goals for the New Year. At first, I was surprised to find that my friend—a smart, educated, and experienced guy—didn't know how to set an effective goal. But the fact was, like most people, regardless of experience or position, he had never been shown how to do so in the most effective way.

What is your gauge for success? While your goals need to be congruent with your vision, each one must be *specific, measurable*, and have a *deadline*. For example, it's not enough to say, "I want to sell more. I want to be happier. I want to make more money. I want to find a great job. I want to develop a loving and supportive relationship." Clarify what success looks like, and write it down.

An example of a specific and measurable goal would look like this: "I want to generate one million dollars in new sales of this product at a profit margin of X percent by 12/31/XX."

Go Do: Set Twelve-Month Goals

Create an appointment with yourself to spend some time thinking about what you want. Write down your personal and professional goals. Follow the guidelines in this chapter to ensure that your goals are in alignment with your priorities and are specific, measurable, and have a deadline.

CHAPTER 5

Create Your Strategy to Attain Goals

Strategy and Action Steps

W hen I enter a destination into my car's navigation system, it provides me several views to choose from. One view shows a simple line from my starting point to my destination. Think of this concept as you visualize achieving your goals. However, the line marking the path from start to finish for you will be the overarching strategies and activities you'll need to build into your daily routine while keeping them in alignment with your goals.

What steps will you need to chart out to reach your goal's destination? Consider your sales process. Let's define a closed sale as being your goal—your destination. You likely already have a clear understanding of what steps you and your people need to take with each prospect to close a sale. Your own personal and professional goals are no different. The strategies you create to achieve your goals work the same way as your sales process does in helping you achieve new sales.

Your strategy is the *how* in the equation—a subset of your goals. How do you plan to move forward toward attaining your goals? (Steps might be to improve the onboarding process for new salespeople; increase one-on-one observation time with your team; develop sales-coaching skills; redefine your sales strategy; expand prospecting and new-business development efforts, to include trade shows, speaking engagements, and cold calling.)

And don't forget about your personal goals! For example, do you want to lose weight, learn to play the guitar, or go on a vacation to Hawaii with your family? As with your professional goals, make sure your strategies are specific and measurable.

Your Activities

Align Your Actions with Your Intentions

Action items are a subset of your strategies. After successfully identifying which strategies will best serve you in achieving your goals, break them down even further into discreet and actionable action items you can build into your calendar, blocking out distinct periods of time for each activity. Learning how, when, and where to focus on activities can be trickier than you might imagine. Many people spend time thinking about how they need to generate greater results, such as increasing their sales volume. The question is, are they spending more time *worrying* about things than actually *doing* something about it?

You can see what they are doing because it's reflected in their calendars!

A client was complaining how slow his business has become recently. I asked him, "On a scale of one to ten, where ten means you're putting in your full effort to build your business and one means you're not engaging in daily activities that generate new business, where do you stand?"

He responded, "I'm probably a four."

I then asked, "How much time are you devoting to sales and revenue-generating activities?"

"Two hours per week."

The next time you feel frustrated because results aren't showing up fast enough, consider that your actions may not be aligned with your intentions. And the best way to ensure alignment is by following the following goal-setting steps.

Goal-Setting Steps

The steps are simple, yet people still struggle with implementing them effectively. To help illustrate the process, let's work through a scenario using a goal all sales managers are familiar with: a quarterly sales quota. Your team size, goal/target, industry, product or service, past performance, and dozens of other variables and key performance indicators will make this example different than your own, but if you're in sales, this example will still make sense.

The specific quarterly goal is selling one hundred units (keep in mind, the manager already went through the steps of articulating their vision and translating it into more specific values and priorities). Here is how they broke down their goal into strategies and action steps:

1. **GOAL:**
   a. Quarterly quota: one hundred units

2. **STRATEGY:**
   a. Hire five new salespeople.
   b. Identify key prospects and targeted accounts.
   c. Increase face time with clients.
   d. Leverage technology to align with sales and coaching/training processes.
   e. Create a healthy coaching and observation cadence.
   f. Increase upselling and cross-selling opportunities.

3. **ACTION STEPS:** (For hiring five new salespeople)
   a. Obtain approval from upper management.
   b. Determine whether to hire all five at once or stagger hiring throughout the year.
   c. Review/refresh the new-hire onboarding and training process.
   d. Review/refresh the salesperson job description.
   e. Create the job posting.
   f. Conduct follow-up calls and e-mails.
   g. Conduct preliminary candidate screenings. (Create a list of all distinct classes of interviewing questions, meeting agenda, expectations, etc.)
   h. Conduct phone interviews. (Develop scripting if needed to ensure consistency.)
   i. Hold first round of in-person interviews.

j. Hold subsequent rounds of in-person interviews.

k. Integrate experiential simulations to assess candidates' full competencies, including presentation skills and verbal as well as written communication skills.

l. Conduct "ridealongs" with a manager or existing rep (if applicable).

m. Finalize background checks, prior job history, and referrals.

n. Make job offers and negotiate contracts.

o. Conduct new-hire onboarding and training.

4. **FREQUENCY and ROUTINE:** (After determining the specific action steps required to implement each listed strategy of your goal successfully, schedule the tasks in your calendar and build out your routine—something we'll discuss at length in the next chapter.)

Goal Tracking

This is not a technology manual. It's entirely up to you which apps, programs, and devices you use to manage your goals and schedule. However, it is crucial that you incorporate a familiar and reliable system for tracking your progress. Otherwise, how will you know whether or not what you are doing is working? What else would hold you accountable to what you committed to? How will you know what the results are? Whether you use a handheld device, a personal assistant, an online calendar, or even a piece of paper taped to the wall, you need to be tracking the results of what your goal's strategies and action items are producing.

Go Do: Develop Your Strategy and Action Steps

Now that you have defined your goals, reference the example above and write down the strategies you are going to implement to achieve your goals. Then write down the specific action items you'll need to engage in to make each strategy a success.

Business is dynamic—always. When you break down your strategy, you'll clearly see a list of activities you need to engage in every day that, compounded over time, will generate the results you want and allow you to achieve the goals you set for yourself, your team, and your company.

It's an old adage but applies today: Consistency in action leads to consistency in results. When you have a strategy mapped out and a series of action steps, along with a reasonable timeline to meet realistic expectations, it's a lot easier to reach your final destination.

CHAPTER 6

Outline Your Routine

If Time Is Money, then Your Routine Is Priceless

N ow is when this process really begins to unfold. This is the time to redesign your routine and challenge your thinking around time management. Be prepared to learn the additional truths about time management—it's not only about big visions, goals, and strategies; it's just as much about learning to master the correct day-to-day activities, communication, and way of thinking that can make the biggest impact.

You're now in a position to follow your North Star. For centuries, travelers have oriented themselves and charted their courses based on their position in relation to the North Star. It's always there—constant and unmovable. Boats, trains, horses, cars, and people on foot move and change their positions, but the North Star is steady and unchanging. You now have your own North Star, and it too will always be there for you—unwavering and completely reliable—ready to be your very own guide and point of reference in all that you do around your personal vision and goals.

Now, bring yourself back to today. What are you going to do about your goals and vision every single day to create what is most important to you?

You have now charted your destination and have begun creating your map—the absolute best path possible you can travel to achieve success. Your routine is your daily road map to achieving your goals with the least amount of effort.

Your Routine Is Where Your Plan Resides

By taking the discreet action items associated with each of your goals and placing them on your calendar, whether one-time tasks or recurring ones, you began creating one of the most powerful time-management tools known to man—a routine. I have coached thousands of sales managers on time management and regularly receive their first visceral comment that routines don't work for them. They wish they did! But their work is just too dynamic and ever-changing to be nicely packaged into a tidy, easily predictable routine.

And therein lies the disconnect. For routines to be transformational in helping you achieve your most important goals in life, they can never be stagnant. They need to be organic and alive! They need to be adaptive, and they need to flow. Learning to develop and work with a routine like this allows you to get into what I like to refer to as the "flow zone." But to get there requires what may be perceived as having to map out a rigid routine. Failing to create an organic and flexible routine is the principal reason so many time-management efforts fail—they fail because people do not take into account the complexities of life and the *externalities* constantly in play. But when sales leaders change how they think about routines and internalize the dual truth around routines, it changes everything. While counterintuitive, a day of specific and measurable activities gives structure to your routine while being infinitely flexible to the ebbs and flows of life that happen daily, even with the best-laid plans. These people truly do end up living happier, more focused, and more productive lives.

An effective routine is never static. That's the point of this paradox: How could you fit something static around something that's always changing? You can't. It's less about creating the perfect routine that never changes and more about how you respond to the new things and changes that unexpectedly show up in life. It's learning to be realistic about what things you can control and what things you can't (something we'll cover in more detail in chapter 10).

Think about why each of these components of your Personal Navigation System are so critical to owning your day and how they relate to each other. Each component supports the other, and you can't effectively create one component until you successfully complete the one that precedes it.

But as you proceed from one step to the next, a beautiful portrait of a meaningful vision, ownership, and achievement begins to form. When executed properly, something as cold and calculated as time management becomes very real and alive, with accountability and purpose pulsing through its veins.

That's why all roads, and your ability to achieve your goals and the results you want most, lead back to self-management. Every action, every reaction, and how much of your very best gets pumped into each day all hinge entirely on self-management. And as a manager, not only is it crucial for you to infuse this approach into everything you do for yourself, it's up to you to ensure that your team is engaging in the right activities that are going to drive the most productivity for them for everyone to achieve their business objectives. One thing is for certain: If you're a people manager, after completing this book, you'll recognize infinite coaching moments to help your people take ownership of their day as well.

Go Do: Add Other Recurring Tasks to Your Routine

In last chapter's "Go Do," you began building your routine by inserting all of the action items you had identified for each strategy associated with your goals into your calendar or tool of choice. Some of those action items are recurring in nature, and others are one-time tasks. But for your routine to empower you to achieve everything you want, you may need to incorporate other recurring tasks as well. Take some time now to incorporate any additional activities into your routine that will help you achieve the sense of accomplishment and harmony you're seeking. And don't worry if you don't feel like you capture everything during this exercise. As you continue to read, I will share many additional concepts and ideas with you that will likely prompt you to continue updating and adjusting your routine even further. Remember, an effective routine is alive, ever-changing, and organic.

Some examples of time blocks that you may want to consider are as follows:

1. Morning regimen
2. Commute time
3. Consistent one-on-one time with each of your children
4. Consistent one-on-one time with each of your direct reports
5. Personal training, seminars, conferences, or workshops to attend
6. Daily self-care regimen
7. Personal/spiritual /thinking/reflecting/ study time
8. E-mails
9. Administrative tasks
10. Meetings
11. Phone calls
12. Business reviews with direct reports or customers

Part One—Summary

1. Personal and Profession Vision

Begin the creative process of designing your vision and the ideal lifestyle you want to create for yourself.

2. Core Values and Priorities

Look at your vision, and write down what values (characteristics, attributes, standards, boundaries, and traits) you need to strengthen or adopt to bring your vision to life.

Look at your values (e.g., bravery, trust, learning, accountability, patience) and identify your priorities in life (e.g., spending time with family, making an impact, learning, solving problems, creating, creating solutions, working with customers, developing a team)

3. Specific and Measurable Goals

Set specific and measurable twelve-month goals (e.g., four hundred sold units) that are in alignment with your priorities and also have a deadline.

4. Strategies to Attain Goals and Action Items

Determine what your strategies (e.g., hire five new salespeople, increase face time with clients) will be to achieve your goals.

Break down your strategy into the action items (e.g., obtain approval from upper management, create a job posting, conduct preliminary interviews) you'll need to engage in to make each strategy a success.

5. Organic Routine

Time-block each distinct action item into your calendar and routine.

Take time to incorporate any additional activities (daily exercise, volunteer time, etc.) into your routine that will contribute to achieving the overall success you desire in life.

[PART TWO]

How to Own Your Day

CHAPTER 7

Assign a Value to Your Time

Achieve More, and Simplify Your Life

To achieve this requires that you begin with engaging in the activities that move you closer to your goals and produce the best results for you with the least amount of resistance.

Because time is our most precious, nonnegotiable commodity, it's essential to invest it in those activities that produce the greatest personal dividends.

As I mentioned in the last chapter, if time is money, then an effective routine is priceless. Take a few minutes to establish a monetary value for your time. Attach a dollar figure to it. What do you feel your time is worth? Regardless of whether you are salary-based or incentive/commission-based, put a dollar figure on what you feel you are worth per hour. For example, is your time worth $50 per hour, $100, $500, or $5,000 per hour?

Scale or Fail?

If you are taking on certain projects, activities, or tasks, then what does that do to the value you have placed on your time? You may find yourself performing duties that may not maximize your revenue simply because you are not maximizing your time's true value. Engage in the tasks that are most congruent with your goals and what you feel you are worth.

At some point in the future, you may feel that the value of your time will increase. For example, in three to five years, you might project that the value of your time will double. If so, here's an exercise for you to take on. Instead of thinking in terms of what you feel your time is worth *today*, consider the dollar amount you believe your time will be worth in three to five years, and use that as the true value of your time today. In other words, start acting and planning as if your time today is *already worth more*. You'll notice a shift in your attitude around how you choose to invest your time.

The result? Once you start thinking in terms of the higher value you have placed on your time, you'll become more sensitive to the tasks you are willing to take on. You will learn to say no when necessary and delegate more with greater effectiveness, and you will start engaging in more selective and worthy activities.

Chief Problem Solver

There's a direct correlation between the value of your time and what you believe your primary role is as a manager. As I discussed in great detail in *Coaching Salespeople into Sales Champions*, to truly thrive as a sales manage you need to give up your role as Chief Problem Solver because that's not your greatest value. But from years of conditioning and experience, unfortunately, managers learn the wrong lesson.

They learn "My value is being the subject-matter expert. My value is my experience."

No. That's only part of your value. Your real value and primary objective as a manager is *making your people more valuable*. And you don't make your people more valuable by making them more dependent on you.

Here's another time-management paradox: *We create what we want to avoid.*

What does every manager want? A team of independent, accountable salespeople. When your direct reports approach you looking for help or advice and rather than ask them their opinion or for a solution, you instead react and serve up the answer, what message are you really sending them every single time they come to you with a problem? The message you're sending is, "If you have a problem, come to me, and I'll fix it for you."

Unfortunately, this creates an atmosphere in which managers are developing teams of dependent sellers. Of course, the real irony is that when salespeople act on the solution or strategy you proposed and that solution fails, who gets to wear the blame? The manager! After all, it was your solution. That's right—you are actually robbing your people of the very accountability that you desperately want to instill in them.

This is a perfect example of a behavior and a way of thinking you will likely want to begin eliminating from your daily routine. Do the math on this one. After attaching a monetary value to your time, you may find that doing the job you hired someone else to do is difficult to justify financially.

Go Do: Value of Time Now and in the Future

Step One: Assign a monetary dollar amount to your time now.

Step Two: Assign a monetary dollar amount to your time based on what you believe your time will be worth in three to five years.

CHAPTER 8

Create Your List of Nonnegotiables

What Is Your Day Filled With?

W hen many people I work with list what they have scheduled in their calendars, they often share something similar to this:

- 8:30 a.m.: Sales meeting

- 11:15 a.m.: Conference call with client

- 1:00 p.m.: Lunch

- 2:30 p.m.: New-salesperson interview

- 4:00 p.m.: Budget meeting

In reality, there is a great deal they're not accounting for in their calendars. Some of the tasks that fill up their day, such as those listed above, would be considered absolutely essential or nonnegotiable, but many would not. Only when you're being realistic with what you're putting in your days can you start the process of checking off, highlighting, or circling the activities that are nonnegotiable.

Some nonnegotiable activities include your commute (if any) or other predefined functions you have to perform at work due to the responsibilities of your job. As a sales manager, these nonnegotiables could consist of sales meetings, scheduled one-to-one coaching sessions, training new salespeople, and even time in the field for observation. Your calendar might more accurately look something like this:

- 5:30 a.m.: Wake up
- 6:00 a.m.: Exercise
- 7:00 a.m.: Breakfast
- 7:40 a.m.: Commute to work
- 8:00 a.m.: Greet team
- 8:15 a.m.: E-mail
- 9:00 a.m. Voice mail
- 9:30 a.m.: Follow up on several projects
- 10:00 a.m.: One-to-one sales coaching
- 11:15 a.m.: Conference call with client
- 1:00 p.m.: Lunch
- 2:30 p.m.: New-salesperson interview

- 4:00 p.m.: Budget meeting
- 5:00 p.m.: E-mail
- 6:00 p.m.: Voice mail

Make Self-Care Nonnegotiable

Even though I have alluded to this already in this book and in other books I've written, the topic of making self-care nonnegotiable is of such critical importance to reaching any goal and is especially relevant to the topic of time management that I felt compelled to include it here as well.

You don't need to wait until the end of the year to reward yourself! Having fun is no longer the by-product of hard work, finishing a task, hitting a quota, or something we reward ourselves with after financial gain. Rather, it's something we can derive from our lives on a daily basis. Unfortunately, this is very difficult to do without a well-structured routine in place!

Let's face it—this is not our practice life! There's no dress rehearsal. The fact is, it's easy to get caught up in this process when you have a clear path to attaining your goals. That's why you need to be proactive and incorporate self-care into your routine. That is time just for you, time for personal and professional development, time to do the things that bring you the *most* joy and maximize your health, and time for self-reflection.

Find some time during the day and throughout your week that is your time, downtime, or do-nothing time. Treat this as sacred time. Even if that means taking an hour break to hit golf balls, go to the gym, meet a friend for coffee, take a bike ride, go for a walk, or read a book, it's time well invested. It will allow you to rebuild your energy level and clear your mind of all the clutter that accumulates throughout the day.

The fact is, to take care of others as effectively and successfully as you can—your team, peers, customers, and family—you need to first take care of yourself. I know this may sound selfish, but consider that it's more about being *self*-ish.

For example, think about when you're traveling on an airplane. The flight attendant goes through the safety protocol before taking off. After they teach us how to use a seatbelt, they say, "In the unlikely event of an emergency, the overhead compartment will open, and an oxygen mask will fall down. Put the oxygen mask on yourself first before helping others." Why? Because you can't take care of others if you don't take care of yourself first.

Aside from exercising, use this time to mentally download all of the things that have transpired throughout your day. Take time to process it all and to embrace what you are learning, where you were, where you are, and where you are going. Otherwise, when do you make the time to decompress or unwind? If you don't treat this as a priority, you may continue to feel like a tightly wound coil ready to snap. Gee, no wonder you may be feeling *off*, overwhelmed, or stressed.

Don't have an hour each day? Then take fifteen minutes. The fact is, we spend about two-thirds of our life working and sleeping. Factor in your other personal responsibilities, and there's not much time left. So ask yourself, "When am I happiest?"

Are you doing the things that bring you the most joy and that take care of you?

Be careful of falling into the all-or-never trap. That is, "Either I'm going to exercise and eat healthy every day or I'm not." Don't set yourself up for failure. Be realistic, and start with what you know you can commit to. Then build on those successes each day.

Expose Your Diversionary Tactics

Some nonnegotiable tasks, activities, and priorities in your life may be obvious; however, some may not be so visible.

The activities you need to engage in that support your lifestyle and will truly determine whether or not you will reach your personal and professional goals need to be nonnegotiable tasks rather than optional. Otherwise, you'll find that they have tendency to take a backseat to the activities or tasks you may be more comfortable doing (such as cleaning your office, doing paperwork, responding to e-mails, helping other people, compiling data, attending meetings, putting out fires, and working on getting your new-hire training material *perfect*) but don't significantly move you forward.

Instead, they'll keep you stuck in maintenance mode, allowing you to do just enough to stay afloat. Then you may have conversations with yourself that sound like, "That's okay; I was busy today. I'll do that tomorrow." Or "I just wasn't able to find the time to get to that today." And wouldn't you know it, something else always seems to come up!

This busy work will disguise the truth, creating the illusion that you're working hard simply because you feel busy. These *diversionary tactics* enable you to do everything but the activities that would dramatically accelerate your success. Just ask any salesperson who has to prospect to build business. They can justify practically any and every activity that will take them away from prospecting, allowing them to major in the minor activities that act as a diversion to doing what's truly needed to build their business.

"Find the time?" In my experience, I have yet to stumble across time I just happen to "find." It becomes a never-ending search, an exercise in futility; "The Journey to Find the Time."

Consider that these nonnegotiable activities must become as habitual as waking up in the morning, taking a shower, brushing your teeth, and breathing. These are the activities you do (hopefully) without a second thought. That's why you must make the time first to do them until they become habitual for you.

Go Do: Schedule Your Nonnegotiables

Schedule an appointment with yourself for self-care. Build this time into your routine, and schedule the activities that you'll do for yourself every day or every week that are just for you. Go a step further, and schedule an appointment with yourself for one full day each month that is just for you. This is your time to have fun, for reflection, to catch up, or to rejuvenate yourself. Doing so will provide you with some well-needed freedom and will make you more effective in every other area of your life.

Chances are, you are only going to get busier. So if you don't make self-care nonnegotiable *now*, it may never make it into your routine later and will end up being the first thing that gets compromised. After all, if you don't do it now, then when is the big payoff?

Other nonnegotiable time blocks you need to consider in your schedule as a sales manager could be weekly scheduled appointments with your direct reports, boss, peers, customers, and cross-functional teams.

Being the optimistic realist, this list might also include those personal responsibilities that don't make the list of making you exceptionally happy but absolutely need to get done for you to achieve your personal and professional goals, and you are unable to eliminate or delegate them to anyone else.

[PART TWO]

CHAPTER 9

Identify Your Value—
Delegate the Rest

Developing Strengths and Delegating Weaknesses

It's time to identify and develop your strengths and delegate or eliminate the activities or tasks that don't support them. Everyone has strengths and weaknesses. Do you know what yours are?

The mistaken belief is that if we spend time strengthening our weaknesses, it will help us grow. But even if you do end up strengthening your weaknesses, you're still likely to only end up with some very strong weaknesses. The irony here is that your strengths are not getting the attention they deserve that made you successful in the first place.

Instead of spending the time strengthening your weaknesses, practice developing your strengths and delegating your weaknesses, surrounding yourself with other great sales leaders. Besides, the people you hire are the future leadership of your organization, right?

Engage in the activities and tasks you are really good at. Focus on strengthening your personal talents, gifts, and abilities. I guarantee there are certain items that you can let go of or take off your plate and give to someone else. That's why the Go Do at the end of this chapter contains one of the most important exercises of the book—to determine the tasks or activities you can delegate that have to be done but are not the best use of your time or don't maximize your strengths. After that, you will determine who is the best person to delegate these tasks to.

As a sales manager, it's critical that your role and the responsibilities of each person on your team are clarified and that you are allowing your people to do their jobs. This will eliminate any overlap or redundancies and ensure that each person is accountable around effectively contributing to the overall success of your team.

How to Delegate Safely and Effectively

Everyone wants more time, and delegation is one way to create it. Yet, we often have a hard time letting go, believing that we are the best person to handle the task to have it done correctly. Become a more powerful and less frustrated sales leader by learning the following ten simple steps to safe and effective delegation so that you can get your day back and focus on the things that matter most.

Sales managers are often left feeling frustrated when their staff members don't perform tasks the way they expected. Then, quite often, managers learn the wrong and dangerous lesson: "If you want something done right, you have to do it yourself." We often lay the blame on the people we delegated to, believing they are not competent and fail to meet your expectations and achieve the results you desired.

Stop and think about who would ultimately be accountable for any breakdown during the delegation process. Yes, it's the person who delegates the task. To eliminate communication breakdowns permanently, we must take full accountability not only for the message we send but for the message the other person receives. And that's the good news because now it's 100 percent in your power to create the outcome you want in every conversation.

You can eliminate the frustration that ensues when your people don't follow through and perform the way you expect by sharpening your communication and filling in the gaps that are often left open for interpretation. Here are ten steps for sales managers to delegate safely and effectively.

Step 1

Know what the task is. (Delegate one task at a time. If you emphasize everything, you emphasize nothing.)

Step 2

Have the end result/desired outcome you want to produce in mind. This level of clarity is critical to create alignment around what is expected.

Step 3

Find the right person you need to delegate to, and give her the task.

Step 4

Share with that person the results you desire.

Step 5

Ask her why she feels this task is important. Once you uncover their point of view, fill in the blanks and share with her what she missed— that is, share with her any additional reasons why this task is important, its overall impact, and the role she plays in completing it.

Step 6

Follow up Step 5 by asking, "How can taking on this task benefit you?" What is the advantage for her to handle this project or task? Acknowledge not only her role but also how completing this task or project will benefit her. After all, every person, when asked to do something, try something, or change something, is immediately thinking, "What's in it for me?" Making someone feel needed, included, and part of the team builds their skill set and confidence and helps them do a better job. Simply telling them what to do does not.

Step 7

Ask her how she plans to approach and complete this task. Ask questions such as, "How have you handled something like this in the past?" "How would you go about handling/completing this?" and "What's your opinion about how to resolve this?" The answers to these questions will determine if she is comfortable performing this task and whether or not she has the right tools, information, strategy, skills, and knowledge needed to complete it. It will also help you uncover the gaps in her strategy, should her strategy be half-baked. Now, rather than run the risk of being redundant, you can listen for the gap in her thinking and solution. Then coach her to fill in the gaps or missing pieces that are needed to effectively complete this task, or share with her what needs to be refined in her suggested solution or approach. (Caution: while doing this, be careful not to sound condescending. You can say, "So repeat back what I just told you.")

Step 8

Determine the exact time frame in which you want the task completed. Ask questions such as, "Given your current commitments, when do you feel you can complete this?" This creates ownership in the person's mind to get it done because she is creating the timeline herself. (If the deadline she chooses isn't appropriate, ask, "What would you need to complete this task sooner?")

Step 9

Reconfirm. To ensure crystal-clear communication and alignment in thinking, reconfirm what was discussed. That can sound like, "Okay great, so to reconfirm, you will be able to have _____ done by _____ date?" Or "So I can expect the presentation on my desk by tomorrow at _____?" This will eliminate any costly assumptions or misinterpretation of the message on both sides, as well as clarify your expectations.

Step 10

Most important, make sure you follow up at the time the task was to be completed to ensure it was done. Otherwise, you run the risk of sending the wrong message to your direct report. If you don't follow up, your direct report will be thinking, "Well, my boss didn't follow up with me, so it seems this wasn't that important after all. I guess it's okay not to complete what's asked of me because there's no consequence anyway."

With no follow-up, you're giving your people the out so they do not have to be accountable for completing what is asked of them. Now they believe it's okay for tasks not to be completed!

Remember, *you can't scale dependency*. To focus on the more timely and important projects, tasks, and goals requires letting go of being a control freak and trusting the people you work with. Otherwise, you'll find yourself in a position where you're not only doing your job, but now you're taking on everyone else's job and responsibilities. Following these ten steps to safe and effective delegation will help you build further accountability, confidence, and trust within your team and with those you have to influence. It also will help you maximize your skill set and leverage your time to focus on the activities and results that serve you best.

Go Do: Delegate Something Now

Using what you learned from this chapter, identify three tasks you are currently responsible for that would be better handled by someone else on your team. Identify another three tasks you're not responsible for but handle anyway. Delegate those tasks to the appropriate people/person using the ten steps listed above.

CHAPTER 10

Treat Everything like an Appointment

Your Calendar Is Lying to You

B ottom line: If it takes up time, then consider it an appointment and schedule it.

Getting ready in the morning, breakfast, and your commute to work are just some of the activities that need to be part of your routine. Treating every activity as an appointment will allow you to plan better. It will also keep your honest about how much time you actually have throughout your day so you can realistically assess what you can and cannot do so. That will help you perform each task with conscious intention.

Here's a rhetorical question: Have you ever been in a situation in which you promised more than you could deliver?

That's right—you overcommitted yourself!

There are three primary causes that lead to overcommitments, and if you think it's a strategic issue, then you are off. In fact, they're all rooted in not having an honest relationship with time:

1. Not being realistic with how long each task or project will take
2. Not planning for unplanned externalities (upset clients, sick salespeople, traffic, longer meetings, additional e-mails, unexpected calls, etc.)
3. And finally, not being realistic with what you already have scheduled in your day (getting ready in the morning, breakfast, or your commute to work)

If it takes up time, then consider it an appointment and schedule it. Think about how having an honest handle around how much time you actually have each day so that you can effectively plan out your routine will keep you when it comes to the commitments you make.

For example, before you had a realistic routine in place, perhaps things unfolded something like this:

Salesperson: "Boss, I really need your help! Are you available for a deal review at three o'clock this afternoon?"
You: (After looking at your blank calendar) "Sure, I've got time. See you at three. "

After developing a more honest relationship with time and creating a more realistic representation of your routine in your calendar, that same scenario could possibly unfold like this:

Salesperson: "Boss, I really need your help! Are you available for a deal review at three o'clock this afternoon?"

You: (After looking at your thoroughly filled-out calendar) "I'm actually joining another salesperson on a conference call with one of our biggest clients at that time, but I'm free at one forty-five, two fifteen, or four o'clock. Would one of those times work instead?"

If you don't have the appointment, you don't have the commitment.

There's No Such Thing as Free Time

That's right—there's no such thing as free time because everything, including what you would do during your free time, needs to be scheduled. This includes downtime; time to process, reset, and refocus; meditation time; and time for self-reflection. I know it may sound strange, but if you're not scheduling these things into your routine, then chances are, you're not doing them or doing them consistently. And if you're not taking the time to schedule your free time, here's an opportunity to do something the world's top leaders do.

Go Do: Make Your Calendar Honest

First, review any to-do lists you have, and transfer those tasks into your calendar, or at least block out time for when you plan on working on certain groups of tasks. We explore this at a deeper level later.

Second, take a moment and make a list of any other tasks that you tend to keep track of in your head. Once you have those all written down, insert them into your calendar as well to help create a more accurate representation of your day.

.

CHAPTER 11

Be Realistic with Your Time

Plan for the Worst

While some may have tried, it's impossible to play a great round of golf in an hour. It's also impossible to drive from New York to California in six hours. If you have a meeting across town that is thirty miles away, instead of assuming you'll be able to make it there in twenty minutes based in the best-case scenario, for your integrity and peace of mind, plan for worst-case scenarios instead.

Three Steps to Completing Your To-Do List Every Day

Now that you have captured every imaginable activity and action item and made them a part of your routine, you will want each activity to be scheduled for appropriate and realistic lengths of time. Use the following guidelines to determine how much additional time to add on to the timelines you have created for each activity.

1. For the tasks/activities you have never engaged in before and are not sure how long they will take, *double* the timeline you have allocated for those tasks/activities. (Example: If you had originally allocated one hour for an activity, now allocate two hours.)

2. For the tasks/activities you have engaged in before and have an idea how long they will take but are not completely certain, *add 50 percent* to the timeline you have allocated for those tasks/activities. (Example: If you had originally allocated one hour for an activity, now allocate 1.5 hours.)

3. For the recurring tasks/activities you know you have only a finite amount of time to engage in or are pretty confident in how long they truly take (prospecting, going to the gym, taking a bike ride, e-mails, reading the newspaper), *leave them alone* for now.

After discussing this strategy with one of my clients, she said, "If I add even fifty percent to each activity per day, my day would end at ten in the evening rather than five in the evening, which it winds up doing anyway!"

Herein lies the greatest lesson. If that's the case, then you have too much on your plate. Hey, it's up to you to accept this hard truth or not.

The intention of this chapter is to honor the timeline it takes to finish something so you are able to complete these tasks once they are part of your routine rather than always running out of time and leaving them incomplete.

Facts:

- You can't safely drive from New York to Washington, DC, in two hours.
- You can't play a great round of golf in an hour (eighteen holes).
- You can't train for one week and expect to be in great physical shape.

The point here is, if you have a ten-hour work day, you can't effectively complete ten hours of tasks in that time period, even with all your good intentions. So if you look at what you normally have in your schedule and then total up the time it would realistically take to complete your daily to-do list, I'm sure you'll see a disconnect between the hours you invest in your typical work day and the time it would take to complete your daily tasks.

You have a choice to make. If you follow this strategy, you will likely continue beating yourself up, feel guilty about what you are not getting done, and make yourself feel bad for not completing what you said you would, even when completing those tasks was impossible from the start with your best efforts at play. If this tactic isn't working for you or enhancing the quality of your life, then commit to changing to a better more realistic approach today.

To recap, you can continue to pile on more activities and tasks that you won't get to anyway, which will make you feel bad for not completing them at the end of day. Or you can begin to underpromise to others and to yourself by putting realistic timelines on your calendar and the activities you engage in so that at the end of day, you feel great for accomplishing what you said you would in a productive, realistic way!

Setting up your routine using time blocking as outlined in this chapter makes it possible for you to determine what you can and cannot do. It forces you to be honest with the time you have available. This way, you can prioritize your tasks and engage in the ones that best serve you.

When you realize how little time you actually have, you will become more sensitive to what you're putting in your day and will increasingly appreciate how valuable your time actually is.

Once you get used to this process, you'll be amazed and excited about the results you'll experience, especially in terms of how you feel. This will also provide you with the opportunity to actually breathe throughout your day.

After all, what's the worst that can happen? Instead of running out of time, you'll actually be running into it!

Go Do: Take Three Steps

Work through the "Three Steps to Completing Your To-Do List Every Day" as detailed in the beginning of this chapter. This will help ensure that you have allotted sufficient time to complete the tasks on your calendar realistically while knowing how to manage other people's expectations.

CHAPTER 12

Determine the Best Time For Each Activity

Be Mindful of when You Are Operating at Peak Performance

D etermine the most appropriate time for the activities you engage in by first uncovering when your peak productive hours are. By now, you know exactly which activities you need to be engaging in. Now it's time to ensure that you are engaging in those activities at the absolute best times throughout your day and week.

For example, being on social media or reading a magazine during peak business hours or during prime prospecting hours is probably not the most effective use of your time. Peak productive hours are for engaging in the activities that you have deemed a priority. So they need to be done at certain times during the day.

Which activities from your action-item lists or other nonnegotiables require you to interact and collaborate with others (e.g., one-on-one coaching sessions, team meetings, client calls)? What part of the day would be ideal for others who are involved to participate in these activities?

Now that you have identified which activities during your peak productive hours would be best to engage in, try to schedule those activities during the time when you are operating at peak performance. When are you at your best?

Some creative people find that they are most creative in the morning hours. So for them, scheduling time in the evening to develop new marketing pieces or to write a new blog post may not serve them best. The creative juices for others don't seem to start flowing until after 10:00 p.m. Everyone is different. It's crucial to know when you work best and plan accordingly. Some prefer exercising at 4:30 or 5:00 a.m., while others prefer to do so after dinner. Honor your personal rhythm of when you function at optimal performance.

I realized years ago that I do my best work in the morning, so I start my day at 4:45 to 5:00 a.m. That's when I engage in the more creative work and the writing I need to do. I also know that I'm not one who can exercise in the evening, so I also make sure I plan my exercise and workout regimen in the morning hours as well.

When Do You Schedule Your Coaching?

What about coaching your direct reports? Outside of situational coaching conversations, which can happen throughout the day, when do you schedule your coaching sessions with your direct reports? And what if the time you want to coach them doesn't align with when they want to be coached? Even though you may be able to recognize when you are at your best for each activity, sometimes you may not be able to get that in perfect alignment when others are available or the times that work best for them. Use the tools you have as a coach to prepare for each scheduled one-to-one coaching session to maximize every coaching session.

E-Mail, Texts, and Phone Calls

More distractions are being created daily that become our greatest temptation and greatest nemesis. This includes apps, texts, e-mails, phone calls, or anything else that keeps your eyes glued to your phone or computer screen.

Now, imagine yourself focused on writing an important e-mail response to a client. Your phone beeps. A text is coming in. At that moment, you have a choice. You choose to shift the focus of your energy and thoughts from the e-mail you were working on to the incoming text. Inefficiency ensues, and the text is taking up time. Whether it's ten seconds or ten minutes, that time is compounded over days, months, and years.

For example, let's say that for every five minutes you check your incoming e-mails, you are losing one minute. That's twelve minutes per hour. In a ten-hour workday, consider that you are *losing at least two hours every day from unproductive distractions!*

If you are a sales manager who is also tasked with certain kinds of creative responsibilities in addition to managing a sales team, consider that creating a marketing piece or writing an article requires a different mind-set than answering a phone call, creating a presentation, preparing a quarterly report, or replying to an e-mail. Allowing certain interruptions will surely stall or block your focus and flow of creativity, affecting your level of productivity. Imagine trying to play golf, tennis, and baseball at the same time!

Consider this solution. Turn off all desktop and phone e-mail notifications, and then schedule set intervals for when you will open and check your e-mail. Depending on your situation, effective intervals for checking e-mail can range from every fifteen minutes to every four hours. While this may sound excessive, I've heard of some people treating their response time to e-mail like regular postal/snail mail. That is, with less frequency since your regular mail is only delivered once a day.

Sure, e-mail is a great tool for communication, collaboration, and correspondence, enabling us to communicate quickly and conveniently. The point here is to ensure that this tool continues to be productive and efficient for you, without consuming your life.

Managing your e-mail like snail mail may sound challenging for your situation. Trying to check your e-mail only once every four hours can feel like an eternity to some people.

One expectation we have established regarding internal e-mail communications at Profit Builders is that no e-mails are inherently urgent. If we send someone else an e-mail, we don't expect that e-mail to be replied to immediately, and we know that the recipient understands that as well. An unwritten rule we have established is that if an e-mail is urgent and requires immediate attention, then we will send the other person an accompanying instant message or text requesting that they look at their e-mail and reply. While this may appear to be inefficient because it requires sending two communications instead of one, we have learned that very few e-mails are actually urgent, and by not demanding instant responses, an occasional extra few seconds sending an instant message more than makes up for needing to constantly monitor and reply to e-mail.

As you work on determining you own e-mail strategies, ask yourself these questions:

- "Are most of my e-mails time-sensitive? Does my ability to respond to an e-mail quickly determine whether or not I will earn a new salesperson's trust and thrive as a sales manager? Is it possible that this is a costly assumption?"

- "Can I still provide the same level of support and coaching to my team and not compromise my ability to be available to them or perform my job effectively if I respond to e-mails at certain intervals during the day?"

- "What type of hybrid solution can I create that would work for best managing my incoming communication while setting the proper expectations with my team?"

If creating blocks of time to respond to e-mails or phone calls would compromise your ability to do your job effectively, then this strategy may not work for you. However, if you have a degree of flexibility in your job, consider this. Instead of checking and responding to e-mails and phone calls every four hours, make it two. If two hours still doesn't work for you, try doing so every hour or half hour.

Go Do: Develop an E-Mail and Phone Call Strategy

Determine at what intervals you will be checking your e-mail (e.g., instantly, every four hours, every two hours, every hour, every thirty minutes) and schedule it into your routine/calendar.

The fact is, even if you change the frequency of when you check your e-mail from every five minutes to every ten minutes, you have just cut the time you can lose from this diversionary tactic *in half!*

This same strategy can be used for telephone calls. Consider blocking out time throughout your day to do so. Whether it's once, twice, or three times a day, allocate a designated block of time to make or return calls.

Here's another thought: Take the next week to determine if there's a specific time throughout your day when you receive the bulk of time-sensitive e-mails and phone calls. There still may be an opportunity for you to block out designated times for responding to calls and e-mails at less frequent intervals than you are doing now.

[PART TWO]

CHAPTER 13
Plan for the Unplanned

Build In Automatic Buffers

One thing all people struggle with is managing their time well enough to end each day feeling productive rather than frustrated when looking at a long list of to-do's that were left incomplete. In this chapter, I share a secret to getting everything done each day—without the stress.

You can be the most talented sales leader on the planet, but regardless of how talented you are, either you own your day or your day owns you. And if you're the type of person who feels a bit out of control when it comes to time management due to the things you feel you can't plan for, here's how you develop a healthy, daily routine that will enable you to end your day feeling satisfied and productive rather than stressed and overwhelmed.

I want to revisit the list of three reasons we find it so challenging to adhere to our schedules or complete our to-do lists that I shared in chapter 10:

1. Not being realistic with how long each task or project will take
2. Not planning for unplanned externalities (e.g., upset clients, unplanned meetings, a change in project scope)
3. And finally, not being realistic with what you already have scheduled in your day (such as getting ready in the morning, eating breakfast, or commuting to work)!

In this chapter, we'll be focusing on the externalities in number two above. "Externalities" are things we don't necessarily plan for. They often go unnoticed and fly under our radar screen when we are attempting to map out our week. They have a tendency to eat up our days.

These externalities can also be things like additional time on the phone; traffic; a project or proposal you're responsible for that has a rapidly approaching deadline; a conversation with a customer or coworker; meetings; a timely problem you need to handle; a request from a peer, boss, or direct report that needs to be handled immediately; and e-mails that take on a life of their own.

Many of these things blindside us because they're outside our direct line of vision. Then we wonder why we're often unable to finish everything that's on our plate for the day.

Now, because we don't have a crystal ball to inform us about the imminent things that would unknowingly consume part of our day, imagine if you were actually able to plan for these externalities; these same tasks that often go left unplanned? What if you actually planned for the unplanned?

Learn to Plan for Distractions

One of my clients was a bit resistant to this idea. She shared with me that once a new client hires her company and procures her services, the unplanned begins happening immediately. Irate customers call in, and people want things addressed and handled yesterday.

This client is in the emergency restoration business. So the only time she gets emergency calls is when people have experienced a major or minor disaster such as a fire or flood! As you can imagine, it's probably hard to plan when she will be receiving these calls.

When the calls come in, customers are harried, upset, fearful, angry, or uncertain. And every time my client received a call like this, she would act surprised, as if it were the first time she had ever experienced it! "I can't believe this is happening again" would be her typical reaction. "The phones are ringing nonstop!"

When I asked her how long this has been going on, she said for fifteen years—ever since she started her business.

This would be similar to a doctor who works in the ER and is continually shocked at the number and degree of emergencies that come through the door, saying, "What? Another emergency?"

The solution for this client was apparent. Instead of resisting the truth, she began to embrace it, and the truth was; this is her business! She is in the business of providing not only solutions to her customers' restoration nightmares but providing support, guidance, and reassurance that it will all work out okay.

Instead of being continually shocked at how her customers react when calling her, by embracing this as part of her business and accepting the truth, she was able to more effectively plan for it. She began to make the shift from being highly reactive to responsive and service oriented by anticipating these situations and raising the bar on creating the ideal customer experience, rather than being shocked when they occur.

Embrace Consistent Inconsistency

Here's an exercise worth doing if you want to take back your day. Think about how many hours you work each day. Let's say it's ten hours a day. Now, what most people do is schedule or anticipate that they have ten hours each day to complete tasks, meetings, projects, or activities they intend to get done by day's end.

Now, consider on average how much time you invest in the activities or tasks you didn't plan for, such as the externalities I mentioned earlier. Let's say they equate to three hours each day.

Do the Math

If you work a ten-hour day and three of those are consumed with externalities, or things you couldn't anticipate planning for that need to be handled, then how many hours do you actually have available each day? That's right—seven!

The challenge is, if you ignore this fact because you "have to get everything done," you have a choice to make. You can either embrace this truth and be honest with the amount of time you really have each day and actually build these three hours of externalities into your day, or you can ignore this reality, continue to schedule ten hours of tasks each day into a seven-hour block of time, and then be frustrated and disappointed every day when you don't get everything done.

Many managers admit that the simple act of scheduling everything in their calendars, including blocks of time for unplanned interruptions and inevitable impromptu or situational coaching moments, ends up being the single most important change of behavior they make in their attempt to take ownership of their day. This change allows them to take ownership of their day and finally be able to invest the proper time needed to develop and support their teams.

Build in Buffers (Nonnegotiable)

Some clients tell me that even though they may budget four hours a day in their five-day workweek for the unplanned, one entire day of unplanned events or tasks can show up. The good news is, if you have budgeted your time correctly, then you can use the blocks of time you have allocated for those externalities throughout your week that you didn't use to complete the other tasks that went unfinished during that one day of unplanned activities. This is yet another example of how an effective routine is a living, organic process and personal operating system.

Conversely, if no unplanned events show up until Friday, then as long as you have invested your time wisely during the time you have allocated for externalities, your schedule will balance out.

Finally, if you happen to experience a week with no externalities and it seems as though you have some extra time in your day, congratulate yourself for planning effectively and consider that you are ahead of the game! However, make sure that you are engaging only in the activities that are scheduled in your routine—nothing else. This isn't the time to start dumping more tasks on your plate. If you notice that you consistently have some extra time in your schedule, then you might consider adding something else into your routine that will increase your current productivity and well-being while also moving you closer to making your personal and professional vision a reality.

Planning for the unplanned will accelerate your productivity and enable you to experience the joyful sense of accomplishment that comes from completing the tasks you schedule each day.

Go Do: Build in Your Buffers

Take five minutes to determine how much time each day you realistically spend on unplanned externalities. Schedule that time into your daily routine to create the essential buffer time you need to be able to complete the planned tasks you schedule each day.

CHAPTER 14
Know Your Stop Time Each Day

Embrace the Principle of Enoughness

S *pecific and measurable actions produce specific and measurable results.* In addition, it may help if your tasks, as well as the results you are seeking, are specific and measurable so you know when you have completed them. For example, if your goals were to improve your coaching skills, map out critical conversations, and better develop your people or prepare them for change, then make sure you have narrowed down these intentions so they are specific and measurable.

As a manager, what would be a specific and measurable action to take? How about doing thirty minutes of observation with each of your ten inside sales reps by the end of the day? Is this specific? Yes, your specific action is sitting down with all of your sales reps while they make calls and observe how they perform. Is it measurable? Of course.

Because you have decided to observe each salesperson for the measurable amount of time of thirty minutes each, it will be easy to determine when the specific action will be completed.

Now, think about the result. The result we are looking for is not a vague result but a specific and measurable result. After taking this action, you will be able to measure the result, which will be a list of observations and feedback you will be able to provide your team to help them achieve what's most important to them in their role as salespeople. By taking the specific measurable action of observing each of your salespeople for thirty minutes, you have generated the specific measurable result of a certain amount of feedback for each of your salespeople to keep them at their best.

Quick Summary:

- Observing your people = vague.
- Observing each salesperson for thirty minutes in one day = specific and measurable.

While some tasks can be measured, some cannot. So if you have allocated thirty minutes to reading industry news and updates to keep up with trends in the marketplace, that's it. Don't get caught up in having to finish it every time (unless the task has a deadline) to the point where it consumes you and becomes an all-week activity that takes you away from your other, more important responsibilities.

Know Your Stop Time Each Day

Creating specific and measurable activities to focus on as a sales leader will allow you to stop working at the end of the day at a time you choose because you can trust that those activities will produce the results you're looking to achieve. You won't feel the need to check your e-mail one more time or check just one more report. When you have a well-crafted routine, you'll be able to trust the process.

Know When Enough Is Enough

Achieving your goals and exceeding your monthly sales quota will be the result of the cumulative efforts you make and the activities you engage in every day. When you're mindful of the process, you have the opportunity to recognize and celebrate your accomplishments on a daily basis (even the little ones) rather than pushing for or waiting until "the end." (When do you ever get to "the end" anyway?)

Go Do: Specific and Measurable Review

Take a moment to review you action items, activities, and components of your routine. Assess whether or not they are specific and measurable. Make adjustments as necessary.

CHAPTER 15

Manage Your Calendar like a Puzzle

Flexible Predictability

I f you are still resistant to the strategy of time blocking, that's perfectly normal. Some people tell me they don't like creating blocks of time because they're always running into other priorities or responsibilities that pull them away or conflict with the activity they've allocated for that time.

Realize that having a routine doesn't mean you have to complete your daily tasks every day at the same time (unless they are on your list of nonnegotiables you created in chapter 8).

Imagine a jigsaw puzzle. Now, imagine that each piece in the puzzle is completely interchangeable. That is, all of the pieces are the exact same shape and size. They are also identical in color. Each piece has no picture. Instead, each piece is a solid color—let's say blue. So regardless of where you put the pieces in the puzzle, the final picture will always be the same.

Now, consider your routine. You know your routine is effective if it resembles the puzzle I just described. If planned correctly, your routine will be fluid and flexible, providing you with the freedom to move around the blocks of time you have allocated for designated activities on each day. No matter where you move them, they will still fit into your day. This is what it means to have an organic and flexible routine.

As long as you have time blocked effectively and are being realistic with what you can put into a day, you will be able to enjoy the benefit of moving around the pieces of your day without experiencing any fallout or incomplete tasks.

In other words, your routine is not changing. What you have planned for and what you will have achieved at the end of the day is not changing. All that's changing is *when* you are doing different activities in your routine. For example, you may have scheduled time in the morning for team meetings and planning and time in the afternoon for observation and sales coaching. You then get a call from your boss's boss, who lets you know that she would like to meet with you and your team but has only one opportunity this week to meet with you.

So you simply move the pieces of the puzzle around, using your morning time block for observation and sales coaching and your afternoon time block for a team meeting with your boss. You are simply swapping the time blocks you have created in your day without having to worry about experiencing any consequence. That includes the time block for unplanned activities.

If you are a creative type who feels that having a routine means rigidity, structuring your routine like a puzzle will make it possible for you to retain that degree of spontaneity and independent thinking while engaging in the tasks that support your goals. This will also enable you to become more responsive and flexible, especially when those externalities show up.

Go Do: Puzzle-Piece Sticky-Note Exercise

Get a set of sticky notes, and use about six of them (keep the number even and manageable to start). On a board or wall that you look at every day, use the sticky notes to create five columns, one for each workday, in the shape of a square. Another option to do this exercise is to use one piece of paper or, if you prefer an electronic version, a spreadsheet. Make five columns, one for each day of the workweek, (you can add the weekend later on), with a minimum of six empty blocks of time in each column.

In the middle of each sticky note which represents an empty time block, write down one of your nonnegotiable activities, and place that sticky note at the time you will be engaging in that activity. Make sure you have a designated sticky note for each activity. Finally, write down or block out how much time you are devoting for each one of these activities.

Make sure this first draft of your routine is in your constant line of sight for at least two weeks. This will serve as a reminder that you do have flexibility in your day while ensuring that you're honoring your priorities or nonnegotiables rather than getting frustrated or feeling overwhelmed when you have to make adjustments to your routine.

Remember, if you need to move time blocks or adjust how much time you need to devote to each task based on a more realistic assessment of how long certain activities take, you're simply swapping puzzle pieces and changing the amount of time you blocked out for each activity. That's why I suggest starting out with only *six* of your priority activities per day, so that you can see how much time you have in your day for other tasks and activities. Regardless, when you move the puzzle pieces around each day and allocate the proper amount of time for each activity as well as for buffer time, you will see that everything will still get done for the day.

CHAPTER 16

Create Alternate Daily or Weekly Routines

A Contingency Plan for Your Routine

T his is probably one of the top concepts for sales managers—especially for those who are on the road frequently.

If you are in a position where your location or responsibilities change from day to day or week to week, then develop an alternate daily or weekly routine. As you begin implementing effective time-management strategies into your day, you will notice how some weeks simply won't align well with your routine. Consider the manager whose schedule may experience a sizable disruption such as afour4-day business-trip to meet with reps in the field. You will need an alternate routine ready to plug in for times such as these.

Create an alternate daily routine that incorporates even greater flexibility than your standard routine so that you can use it when needed. It may even make sense to create an alternate weekly routine for times when you will be required to work under significantly different conditions for several days on end. As such, when things change on short notice, you won't need to abandon your routine. You will be able to enjoy the benefits of working with a routine—even during days that would have historically caused you to abandon your routine and just wing it.

I might be delivering a training program or worship services for four or five consecutive days. If I'm focused only on my deliveries from 8:00 a.m. until 6:00.p.m., then I have no choice but to create an alternate travel routine that's realistic and productive.

Be Creative with Your Time

After spending time with my family in the evening, I often catch a second wind and find an extra hour to get some work done rather than watch television. As long as it doesn't take time away from your family or self-care or subtract from your quality of life, keep an eye out for some additional productive time during your day.

Keep in mind; I'm not suggesting operating on two to three hours of sleep. This falls under honoring a healthy, self-care regimen that your mind and body need to function at your best. I function well with six to seven hours of sleep a night, but if necessary, I can get away with five hours of sleep per night for a certain period of time, such as when I am traveling.

Plan for Time to Plan and Think

"Great runners may be born, but they have to learn how to walk first." The point is, the training and planning needed to prepare for the race will always take longer than the race itself. The same holds true for attaining the results and the level of productivity and harmony you are looking for.

How much time do you invest each week to plan? Take the time to plan your week. Forecast what your week will look like. Whether that means putting aside thirty minutes Sunday night or Monday morning, use this time to plan your routine or develop your list of what needs to be accomplished during the week and ensure that you schedule it into your calendar.

Ideally, the majority of your routine will consist of recurring appointments because most of your weeks are consumed with similar activities (e-mail, commuting time, coaching and development, selling and prospecting, administrative time, phone calls, meetings, personal time, family time, externalities, etc.). The more consistent your routine becomes, the less planning time you need every week.

Go Do: Create Your Plan B, and Plan to Plan

Create your alternate daily or weekly routine. Keep your alternate routine close by so you can plug it into your calendar quickly and easily as an alternate calendar. With today's smartphones, tablets, calendar applications, and customer relationship management (CRM) software, you can create two versions of your routine and choose which one you will follow for that week.

Because this is an activity that takes time, schedule a block of time into your routine for weekly planning. Just like a runner schedules the time to train so he can finish his race in the shortest amount of time, planning in advance will save you valuable time, help you avoid redundancies, increase efficiencies, and prevent countless headaches throughout your week that result from externalities.

Part Two—Summary

1. Assign a Value to Your Time

Determine what monetary value you'd attach to your time now and in three to five years.

2. Create Your List of Nonnegotiables

Make self-care nonnegotiable. Build these nonnegotiable tasks into your routine.

3. Identify Your Value—Delegate the Rest

Develop your strengths, and delegate your weaknesses. Find the person or people to delegate to. Delegate effectively using the ten steps provided.

4. Treat Everything like an Appointment

Your current calendar may be lying to you regarding how much time you truly have in a day for unplanned activities. Just think of all the seemingly insignificant things or habitual things you do every day that take time from your day. If you don't have the appointment, you don't have the commitment. If it takes up time, schedule it. Therefore, everything gets scheduled.

5. Be Realistic with Your Time

Plan for the worst-case scenario. Complete the three steps provided to ensure that you're allocating the proper time needed to complete each essential activity.

6. Determine the Best Time for Each Activity

Be mindful of when you are operating at peak performance. Develop a new strategy for when and how often to check and respond to e-mails.

7. Plan for the Unplanned

Build in automatic buffers. Plan for distractions. Embrace consistent inconsistency. Honor the mathematical equation of how much time you actually have to proactively plan for activities, projects, tasks, meetings, and other commitments.

8. Know Your Stop Time Each Day

Embrace the principle of enoughness. Make your routine specific and measurable so that you feel a sense of accomplishment at the end of each day.

9. Manage Your Calendar like a Puzzle

Thrive by learning to move the activities in your routine around like identical puzzle pieces. This will give you more freedom and confidence throughout your day because you know you will be able to accomplish what's most pressing and important. Adopt the belief that there is no such thing as a "perfect" routine. Like you, your calendar will evolve and change over time.

10. Create an Alternate Daily or Weekly Routine

Create an alternate routine or a contingency plan for your routine so you can easily switch to your alternate routine, especially when you travel.

[PART THREE]

Live Responsibly

CHAPTER 17

Multitasking Is Evil

Eyesight, Foresight, and Insight

It's no shock that the majority of managers I run into are smart people. They are some of the most driven, optimistic, and high-energy people I've had the privilege of working with, and so are their salespeople. These managers have historically been the top producers and highest achievers within their companies. Their passion, spirit, values, commitment, competitiveness, and purpose fuel their efforts and are the driving force behind what made them successful in the first place.

But to those who observe a manager's behavior, her drive and productivity can be misleading, implying that she is doing or can do several different tasks at the same time. Managers are often considered to be master multitaskers.

Based on what you've observed, is there a universal definition of "multitasking" in your company or on your team? Trust me—there's a distinct difference between what is universally agreed on and true and what we have observed or experienced. And based on this truth alone, we each have our own distinct definition of *multitasking*.

The real problems begin when sales leaders start to believe in the illusion that they are masterful at multitasking and that it's actually necessary to get the job done.

Think about what multitasking might look like while engaging in a conversation with one of your direct reports. Let me set up the visual for you.

It's after lunch, and you're walking down the hallway, heading back to your office. One of your salespeople grabs you and begins filling you in on a meeting he just had with prospect. It's about a deal he's been working on for the past several weeks. You walk together until you reach the door to your office. In the middle of asking your salesperson about an objection he mentioned struggling with, the desk on your phone begins to ring. You let it ring twice when you notice a text message from your boss on your mobile phone.

What are you thinking at this point? Right now, right here, this situation becomes another one of your defining moments. Do you fall victim to actually believing you're capable of handling these multiple tasks effectively at the same time? Do you hold up your finger and say to your direct report, "Sorry, just one second" while you grab the call? Or do you keep nodding and looking up periodically from your phone, trying to demonstrate to the salesperson at some level that you are engaged and listening while you simultaneously reply to the text you just received?

Look at you! Making it all happen at once. You feel as if you're getting all kinds of things done at the same time. You're so productive! You must feel proud being a master multitasker to get multiple tasks done at the same time. Your direct report must be impressed as he observes you giving him your divided attention.

Are You Building or Eroding Trust?

Or is he? What is he really thinking at this point? "Gee, I guess what I'm doing isn't as important to him as it is to me. Then why did he tell me to do this?" or "His call and text is more important than me." Or worse: "I'm simply not his priority."

It can take months to build the trust needed for any relationship to be successful and only seconds to destroy it. But don't give up hope. You can always rebuild trust by resetting the expectations in any relationship. I spend a whole chapter discussing "the art of enrollment" in my book *Coaching Salespeople into Sales Champions,* which is the language sales leaders use to set or reset expectations, while creating buy-in and alignment around shared goals.

The law of reciprocity always starts with you. When you multitask while engaging in a conversation, task, or project with someone, especially someone on your team, you're doing one of two things in every conversation: You're either building trust, or you're eroding it. You are either developing or supporting someone, or you're not. Multitasking erodes trust every time. Period.

Multitasking is evil. In addition to the collateral damage it creates within relationships, it rarely, if ever, works because you are not investing 100 percent of your time, focus, and energy into performing and engaging in each task, activity, or conversation the very best you can.

Instead of trying to do multiple tasks at the same time and achieving only mediocrity with all of them, choose to do just one task or focus on one conversation at a time, and see that through to completion. This way, you can do it with precision and maximum output.

Speaking of the conversations you have each day, keep in mind that self-management isn't just a strategy but a language and way of communicating. If you're resisting this idea, then you'll appreciate chapter 20 regarding adrenaline and your relationship with it.

Attempting to have a conversation with someone while checking e-mail or texting is like trying to play tennis, golf, and soccer simultaneously. You may feel a rush of excitement and adrenaline from doing so, but you won't be playing any sport as masterfully as you could if you were focused on only one.

What's the point of time blocking if you're going to do several things at once and not achieve the level of excellence you're capable of? To take the sports analogy even further, the path to improvement and mastery comes from doing certain drills over and over again to the point of perfection—to the point of developing muscle memory so that you can execute your skills in the game flawlessly and with very little effort or thinking. And this becomes more automatic and natural for you through the process of ongoing practice and refinement.

A good coach would never recommend that you work on several different drills at the same time. So why do we think it's a good idea to attempt running multiple drills on the sales floor at the same time?

Because of the illusion of productivity, often based on what you were taught by your manager. In reality, it doesn't work. Committing to working on a single task at any time is crucial if you want to avoid errors and truly take back your day.

Go Do: Practice Chat

Take a moment right now to practice focusing on a single task. Find someone at home or at work whom you can visit with. The conversation can be work-related but doesn't need to be. Feel free to talk about upcoming weekend plans, a sporting event, a certain project or customer, or something in the news. As you talk, avoid any impulses to check your phone or to engage in any activity other than the conversation at hand. See how long you can go—a minimum of ten minutes.

Notice how focused the other person is during your conversation as well. This is when the law of reciprocity kicks into high gear. That is, if I give you the gift of focus, listening, interest, and attention and I respect your opinion, you in turn will reciprocate that for me. Now, imagine if you create the same type of atmosphere and relationship with each one of your direct reports, peers, and customers. This is what breakthroughs are made of.

CHAPTER 18

Eliminate Your To-Do List

Cut the Cord

It's time to kill your to-do list! That's right! We're getting extreme now. If that makes your skin crawl, how about this: It's time to retire your to-do list. Does that make you feel better? Regardless of how you position it, the cord must be cut—the one thing that feeds you the tasks and activities that you're supposed to be doing and focusing on each day.

It's time to abandon your to-do list and find a new home for those activities because the hard fact is, to-do lists don't provide the kind of focus, structure, and accountability people think they do. In fact, they usually produce the opposite effect because often no deadline is associated with each task.

Most of the time, our eternally growing and never-ending to-do lists just make us feel guilty about what we're *not* getting done each day. So let's get rid of them. I'm going to show you how, along with a much better way to own your day.

Self-Accountability

When discussing people's daily or weekly schedules, they often use terms like routine, projects, appointments, tasks, and to-do lists interchangeably. Let's start with distinguishing between recurring tasks and one-time tasks. An effective routine encompasses a series of important and prioritized activities that are scheduled, recurring, and consistently performed the same way.

One-time tasks are nonrecurring, often difficult to plan or predict (a blown light bulb), and intermittent, and as such, difficult to embed into a routine (externalities).

To illustrate the difference, we'll use a sales leader who's looking to develop an effective sales coaching initiative with his team to help develop all team members to reach their fullest potential, reduce attrition, and bring in more clients. As part of his to-do list, he may have listed "Listen to and observe the sales reps and the conversations they're having with prospects when they are cold calling."

The challenge here is, this activity on his to-do list was never assigned a timeline or completion date, and it was never actually scheduled into his routine. As such, it often gets put aside or forgotten about and replaced with myriad other activities that do get scheduled into his calendar or that pulls him in different directions.

Now imagine that instead of putting this activity on your to-do list, you scheduled it as part of your weekly routine. For example, every morning between 8:00 and 9:00 a.m., when this manager's team was making cold calls, he would begin his day by spending thirty minutes observing and listening to one of his sales reps making calls. He was taking the necessary time with that person to first set expectations and then explain to him in why this is a benefit to him. Once your reps are aligned with your intentions, only then can you debrief honestly and authentically around what you observed and how they can improve. Now, this critical activity that will uncover numerous coaching opportunities to schedule tasks as part of his daily activities, with specific timelines attached. When that happens, he's much more likely to get it done.

The key here is to be able to identify the activities you need to engage in on a consistent basis (daily, weekly, biweekly, even monthly) that support your goals, priorities, and lifestyle.

Conversely, one-time tasks with a finite life span and no measurable degree of repetition or consistency are handled differently. Some examples of these kinds of tasks that are more difficult to plan for include replacing the cracked screen on your smartphone, updating software you use, rearranging your office, taking your car in for service, buying a new desk chair, planning your presentation for your yearly national sales meeting, and so on. The constant, however, is that even these activities need to be scheduled in your calendar or you risk not getting them done or not doing them in a timely fashion.

Look at your routine as an automatic, habitual, and natural way of handling the important things in your life and at work that need to be taken care of on a consistent basis. It's also going to help you handle the items that aren't important but still need to get done. It doesn't require the conscious discipline or thought that one-time tasks on your to-do list require simply because these things will eventually become automatic and scheduled as recurring appointments in your calendar. That will make it much easier to measure and manage.

Your to-do list, on the other hand, is more of a tool to remind you of the additional tasks, appointments, projects, or externalities that need to be done that fall outside of your regularly scheduled activities. But in the spirit of abandoning your to-do list and simplifying your life, we're still going to honor the methodology behind crafting a routine, and as mentioned, schedule these items into our calendars. After all, this does fall under the "Planned for the Unplanned" universal law I discuss in chapter 13.

This alone is reason enough to build in the additional buffer time and plan for the unplanned. Remember, if done correctly, while you may have to shuffle a few time blocks or pieces of the puzzle that make up your routine, even these to-do items need to find a place in your calendar to get handled. As I mentioned, if it takes up time, then treat it as an appointment and schedule it.

After you follow your newly created routine for about a month or two and find that it's working for you, your to-do list will naturally diminish. That's because you are already handling the priorities in your life and are automatically referring to your calendar to schedule these to-do items rather than writing them down on a separate, autonomous list with no due date, timeline for completion, or scheduled time(s) specifically devoted to completing them.

Go Do: Mine Your To-Do List for Potential Recurring Activities for Your Calendar

Scan your to-do list for the one-off tasks that need to be scheduled, and add them to your calendar.

Then identify any other remaining tasks that could be recurring and build them into your routine.

Don't limit this exercise to work-related to-do items. Your routine becomes the powerful and truly transformational tool it's capable of becoming only when it seamlessly integrates all of your most important work-related and personal tasks and priorities into each day (such as the nonnegotiables we discussed in chapter 8).

CHAPTER 19

Stop Focusing on Results

Let the Activity Be the Reward

R ealize that there's always more to do! There's always more that can be done at the office, in your home, or in your life. There's always another call that can be made or another e-mail, text, or social-media post that you can respond to. The key is to recognize that it's a process, so you can truly enjoy the journey. After all, what's the point of eating a piece of chocolate cake—to get to the end or to savor every bite? How about the goal of exercising? To finish your workout or to maintain a level of health, vitality, and personal satisfaction while enjoying the process?

The same holds true for your routine. Know when enough is enough each day so that you can recognize and celebrate your accomplishments on a daily basis (even the small ones) rather than waiting until "the end."

Have you ever been in this situation? "Yes! We hit our quarterly sales numbers and business objectives. Congratulations! High five!" And then what happens? Your reward? The counter resets to zero, and you do it all over again! The quintessential "three-calendar month" is driven by quarterly goals for the company.

If you continue going through the process with your eyes solely focused on the finish line, you'll miss out on the journey. Remember, achievement happens every day. Be careful not to hook yourself onto the future. Enjoy the *process* of reaching your goals.

Paradox: The Result Is the Process

What if you shifted most of your attention away from the result you want or need and onto the process instead? The *how* in the equation is more important than the *what*, or the goal. This is the champion's way of executing the specific steps of the equation. *How* are you going to achieve your goals specifically, and what is the *messaging and communication* process going to *sound* like when you speak to and communicating with your prospects and customers?

After all, you don't *do* the result; you *execute* the process, which *produces* the result as a natural by-product of your efforts. That's the paradox—by honoring the process, you can enjoy the benefit of knowing that you will attain your goals because it's the process that will get you what you want.

A Flawed Model for Success

"Once I make my quota, hit my number, close that sale, get that promotion, help that customer, have more money, solve that problem, *then* I'll be really happy and satisfied and will finally feel successful!"

For how long?

This is a flawed model of thinking because in this scenario, you're *allowing external situations and outcomes to dictate your internal condition, happiness, confidence, and peace of mind.*

The solution: Shift your thinking from focusing on what's *next* to what's *now.*

Be realistic here. Your goals aren't going anywhere. They're set. So why do you feel the need to continually obsess over the results, let them dominate every conversation, and annoy your direct reports about their goals when interacting with them? They know what their goals and numbers are. Do they need to be reminded about them continually?

Many managers harbor deep inside a limiting and toxic belief that tells them, "Focus on the results, and the results will happen faster."

Yeah, right.

Why obsess over the results when it's going to be *what* you do in the moment and *how* you do it that will ultimately produce your desired outcome and become your ultimate formula for success?

Take the Result-Driven Challenge

Would it make you feel better if we validated this right now? Let's test this theory that plagues sales leaders all over the world. Okay, you'll need to do a guided visualization exercise. Are you ready? Begin. (And remember to close your eyes when doing this exercise.)

Think about your goals, commitments, business objectives, or sales targets. Can you envision them? Are they clear in your mind? Okay.

Now, for the next thirty seconds, that's all I want you to think about. Imagine all of your goals in your mind's eye, and focus on nothing else. Ready? Go!

(Thirty seconds later.)

So what happened? Did the result manifest any faster? Are you now closer to achieving your goals?

I don't think so. My point is that continually focusing on the result doesn't help you achieve the results you seek. Paradoxically, focusing on the result becomes the very detriment to achieving your goals because you are no longer focused on the process, the communication, the *how*, the quality of output, your valued customers, or ultimately your own people and peers.

Of course, it is absolutely essential to plan for your future, set goals, and have a clear vision for yourself, your team, and for your organization. However, this needs to be balanced with being in the moment and choosing to live and act with purpose.

Engagement Starts at Home

If you are a leader, that role doesn't stop or start at work or at home. It's who you are. That's probably why I'm so overly conscientious about what I'm modeling for my children every day.

As the proud father of three honor-roll students, the topic of homework, what they learn at school, and its relevance to the "real world" have a tendency to surface every once in a while.

Sometimes they ask me, "Dad, explain to me how this homework is even relevant to what I'll be doing in the future when I get a job or start my own business. I mean, when will I ever need to use this in the real world?"

My response is simply this: "If it's part of your curriculum and what you need to do and learn to get the grades you want and go to the college you want, then it doesn't matter what you're doing. It doesn't matter how seemingly insignificant it is or how many times you've done that task. Regardless of what it is, if you are going to put forth your personal effort, then focus one hundred percent of your energy and effort on what you're doing in that moment.

"Whether it's a task, project, hobby, sports, practice, homework, or even a conversation, put your head into it—and more important, put your heart into it. Whatever it is you are doing at that moment, do it the very best you can because *what* you do is a reflection of you and *who* you are."

Refocus Now! Everything Counts

Here's a universal law that's impenetrable: The habits and choices you made yesterday are what created the life and career you have today. So here's the real opportunity. The habits and choices you make today will create the life and career you have *tomorrow*.

Think about the things that consume your day. E-mails, phone calls, travel, customer meetings, reports, presentations, training, coaching, working with customers, business development, internal meetings, upselling, handling challenges and problems, admin work, project management, team meetings, cross-selling, forecast reviews, deal reviews, performance reviews, getting to decision makers, weekly reporting, proposal writing/bidding, asking for referrals, your own professional development—I can go on and on.

Here's the point: Are you embracing the same philosophy you tell your children? What about the message you deliver to your team? Are you modeling this yourself?

This certainly doesn't suggest becoming a master multitasker.

Miracles Happen When You Pay Attention

It's so easy to go through the motions without the emotion, to treat exceptional results as just another day at the office, to ignore the seemingly insignificant miracles that happen among your team members and with your customers—the remarkable things you do and what your people do every day. How have they have changed, improved, or grown? Do you even recognize when these things occur? And if you do, are you acknowledging them?

Take this one step further. Are you leveraging these moments to coach people around the best practices you want them to engage in consistently so they can replicate their success and refine their processes?

We incur a greater cost when we have both eyes focused on the result. If you continually focus on and live in the future, at some point, you are going to turn around and realize that your life and career have passed you by. Life is what happens in the now, in the present moment.

And if this isn't enough to ignite the fire of change within you, then ask yourself, "What am I modeling? What message am I sending to the people around me, at home for my family, in my community, and at work?"

Ultimately, whatever you're doing in the moment, regardless of what it is; it is the most important thing you are doing at that time. As a leader, if you can model this, think about the message you are sending to the rest of your team and the other people in your life and the impact it will have.

Respect the dualities of life—two conflicting truths that coexist simultaneously. That is, be mindful of the future while being engaged in the moment.

Simply put, be where you stand.

Go Do: Focus on the Process X3

Write down three examples where you recently focused on the results or goals—sales-related or otherwise—instead of focusing on the process.

Then sketch or quickly write out the process for how you are going to achieve each goal. What are the steps? What will you communicate in those steps? To whom? What does the messaging look and sound like across all communication platforms?

Once this is given the attention it rightly deserves, you will notice how much easier your life will become. You will be taking the time needed to build out your process and best practices consciously and to allow the result to happen as a natural conclusion of your efforts.

CHAPTER 20

Get Off the Adrenaline Train

Adrenaline—The Drug of Choice for Sales Leaders

Y ou may have a drug problem. Many people today are hooked on a commonly abused yet elusive drug whose widespread use seems to be flying under our radar. That drug of choice is adrenaline.

It's time to choose a healthier drug—momentum.

The classic symptoms of adrenaline addiction? Saying yes when you mean no. Overcommitting or overbooking your schedule, delivering on exceptionally tight deadlines, or juggling a list of incomplete tasks. Procrastinating until the last moment. Believing you "work best under pressure." Being easily distracted. Deriving enjoyment by seeking out and solving problems.

Consider that an adrenaline addiction may be creating many of the problems, employee challenges, and obstacles, especially to your sales process, that you want to avoid. Tolerating stress, chaos, disorganization, poor planning, lackluster team performance, or undesirable customers create situations that provide the adrenaline rush associated when working on overdrive.

Like any drug, adrenaline has its rewards. On the surface, it may appear that this legal, seductive drug provides a burst of energy to get something done, tackle a project, or meet a deadline. Being superhuman enables you to accomplish more than what a mere mortal is capable of producing.

However, it's more dangerous than we realize. The body produces adrenaline when stressed, in pain, or to protect us from imminent danger. You don't want the drug to control you and dominate your lifestyle. After a day of riding the adrenaline roller coaster, you crash.

Too much adrenaline from other sources (nicotine, chocolate, caffeine, etc.) can also lead to stomach and heart problems, high blood pressure, and anxiety. Aside from feeling drained, burned out, and exhausted, adrenaline lowers your productivity level and sets you up for dips in performance. If you thrive on chaos, it's difficult to maintain your focus, concentration, peace of mind, or mental clarity. If you're a salesperson, a congested mind does not allow for the space to create the best solutions for your customers during a sales call.

If you're overwhelmed with a pile of tasks, then you can't be *present* with or listening to your customers. This affects your ability to follow a sales process, ask the right questions, uncover your customers' needs, and even create or recognize a selling opportunity. This can create enough holes in your selling approach that many promising sales can fall through. To kick the habit, prevent sporadic results, and get off the adrenaline train, shift away from using adrenaline, and start creating the momentum that produces consistent, long-lasting results.

Just Say No—It's Good for Everyone

Are you a "yesaholic?" Do you instinctively say yes first without considering if you can realistically deliver? The irony is, saying yes and not following through creates what you wanted to avoid. That is, letting others down by overcommitting and not delivering can cost you by causing frustration, unhappy employees, disappointing results, lost business, eroded trust, customer dissatisfaction, and even lost referrals.

Before you respond with a start/delivery date on a project or proposal, ask yourself, "Is this something I want to be doing? Do I have the time for it, and if so, when?" In other words, "Are there activities that I've already committed to that take priority?" I'm sure your family would appreciate (be shocked?) if you made it home for dinner a little more frequently.

When my wife and I were in the final stages of building our new home—the 9th month of a 4-month project to be exact, I had discovered that while my contractor did fabulous work, he didn't honor any of his timelines. He said he had been trying to keep me "happy" by telling me what he thought I wanted to hear.

But was I happy that I had to extend my stay in temporary housing? Happy that I was billed every additional month for storage? Happy that I was paying my mortgage and utilities without living in my home? Happy that my wife and I planned our lives (school for three children) around a four-month timeline? No, I was the farthest thing from being "happy." In truth, this project was a thirteen-month project. But he didn't want to tell me that.

You will make more money, have more loyal salespeople, have happier clients, and deal with fewer internal headaches when you always choose to be honest when setting and managing people's expectations. This is the conversational side of time management that I address in *Coaching Salespeople into Sales Champions.*

I'm not suggesting that my contractor was lying by doing something illegal or immoral. The fact is, I trusted him 100 percent. I'm suggesting setting realistic expectations about what you know to be true and then share it with your people, even if they may not like what you're saying. This strategy will always serve you best.

Do you ever say yes when you're better off saying no? Have you made promises you can't keep or struggle to honor? Do you have a hard time telling your team the truth about how long different company initiatives might actually take or exactly what is expected of them when you ask for their participation on different projects? Do you withhold information from your team or your clients that you know they want or need to hear because you are afraid of a confrontation or losing a sale? Do you believe you need to please people for them to like you? Is your schedule frequently overbooked? If so, you may be a "yesaholic."

When you immediately say yes first without thinking about whether you can realistically deliver on that timeline or expectation, I get it—you always have the best intentions in mind. You believe you can "do it all." Yet think about what happens when you promise to deliver on something (completing a project, meeting with a new hire, getting a report out) and you're not able to honor that promise. How does that make you and the other person feel?

Saying no is often perceived as a bad thing. After all, you don't want to say no and fear letting someone down, looking bad, or losing a sale. And saying no to your boss or even peers?

The irony is, if you inevitably say yes all the time to keep everyone happy and don't follow through with your commitments, you wind up creating what you wanted to avoid from the start. That is, you let others down and create stressful situations that cost time and money and cause problems by continually overcommitting and not delivering!

Being honest, setting clear time expectations, and honoring your boundaries (saying no) is a very attractive trait. You'll find that more people will want to work with you because people respect those who deliver on what they promise.

How to Say No

Here's a quick tip from your coach. The next time someone asks you to do something (including promises you make to yourself), give yourself time to process their request by saying, "Let me check my schedule, and I will get back to you at…" or "Thanks for the opportunity. I will consider it and let you know by…" Then ask yourself these four important questions before you respond. (How important are these questions? In terms of a measurable cost, these six questions would have saved my contractor $42,200).

1. "Is this something I have to do?" (It supports my goals, responsibilities, lifestyle, priorities, etc.)

2. "Just because I can do something well, do I take on projects or tasks that aren't my direct responsibility?"

3. "Do I take on tasks that others could be doing?"

4. "Can I meet this person's expectations?"

5. "Do I really have time for this?" (Are there other activities I have committed to that take priority? What sacrifices am I making to commit to both?)

6. "What is a reasonable deadline/expectation I can commit to in the absolute worst-case scenario?" (If you plan for the worst, you wind up building buffers into your schedule that would enable you to handle unforeseen problems while still honoring your commitments. The result? You'll look like a hero!)

Say No, and I'll Respect That; Say Yes, and I'll Expect That

Start practicing saying the word *no*. Give yourself the opportunity and the space to do the things you want to be doing as opposed to filling your days with the things you overcommitted yourself to doing simply because you're in the habit of saying yes to other people's requests. Realize that saying no to others is only half of the equation. I'm also referring to saying no to your own demands as well.

If you are concerned about people's reactions to hearing no or feel uncomfortable about saying no, it's a perfectly normal feeling, especially when trying something new. Just realize there will be a retaining period for you, as well as the people in your life, as they will need to learn how to interact with you in a healthier, more acceptable way.

After all, where do you think they learned how to respond to you in the first place? From you! You are the one who taught the people in your life how they can treat you, talk to you and what they can expect from you by allowing or tolerating (Chapter Eleven) certain behavior.

After saying "no" a few times, you'll quickly get more comfortable with doing so, since your life will become more simplified once you remove some of the unnecessary clutter that results from overpromising. You can then fully be at choice and do what you really want to do with your time—time that you will never get back again.

Do Complete Work

"I've always been a great self-starter but not a good finisher." Sound familiar? Keeping incomplete projects alive becomes another source of adrenaline. Instead of continually stopping and starting something new, commit to seeing each task through to completion before taking on the next one. Once you've cleared out some space as a result of completing one task, you can add another in its place.

How Adrenalized Are You?

If you identify with 50 percent or more of these questions, you may be an adrenaline junkie.

1. I find myself procrastinating tasks until the very last moment and feel that I "work best under pressure."

2. I frequently attempt to "beat the clock" and arrive late to meetings and events.

3. I get juiced or energized from chaos and solving problems or find that it gives me a sense of purpose.

4. The idea of having nothing to do frightens me. I resist boredom.

5. I run out of patience with people, projects, or situations (e.g., standing in line, waiting for something, or during conversations, when results aren't showing up fast enough).

6. I feel everything should happen now! If it doesn't, I lose interest.

7. I feel guilty if I take time off from work and find it challenging to make the time for or enjoy recreation or relaxation time.

8. I find myself continually focused on the future (goals, projects, activities, results, etc.) instead of on the moment or today. I have a hard time being present.

9. My life and workspace are cluttered and unorganized. I have lots of books, magazines, and newspapers I've saved to read and catch up on. I haven't been able to see the top of my desk for a while.

10. I feel that saying no is a bad thing. It's not easy for me.

11. I may be a "yesaholic." I say yes first when I need to say no.

12. My "to-do list never seems to get completed as scheduled and keeps growing!

13. I find that I have loose ends and unfinished projects. I jump from one incompletion to the next.

14. I don't have measurements of success (measurable goals, milestones, or a routine) or recognize my achievements, and I relentlessly strive to achieve more with no end in sight. I don't determine when enough is enough. So it's never enough.

15. I quickly squeeze in my meals while driving, working, or on the run.

16. To achieve my goals, I sacrifice things like personal time with family and friends; time for leisurely, enjoyable activities each day; and self-care.

17. I don't have a mapped-out path or a series of defined and measurable actions that I take daily and weekly to effortlessly move me toward my goals and ideal lifestyle.

18. I find that I produce irregular, sporadic results with a burst of energy or overexertion rather than generating the momentum that produces consistent results from consistent daily actions.

19. I feel depleted or exhausted at the end of a day.

20. I'm more reactive than responsive and allow external situations or circumstances to control my day (vs. having a routine!).

21. I set unattainable goals and place incredibly high expectations on myself.

22. I anguish over making decisions or find myself being indecisive. (This creates mental paralysis and self-doubt vs. exercising choice and trusting myself and the process.)

23. I have a hard time delegating or letting go of certain tasks that someone else can do.

24. If I do delegate certain things, I often do so without clear direction and find that I need to go back and fix or complete the task myself.

25. I overcommit and find myself unable to deliver on deadlines or follow through on the commitments I've made.

26. I'm driven by interruptions. I allow myself to become easily diverted or distracted by situations, new tasks, or people who take me away from what I was initially focused on.

27. I don't have a healthy, rewarding relationship with time. Time is my adversary rather than my ally.

28. I generally don't write things down. I try to manage my responsibilities and tasks in my head.

29. I'm resistant to the idea of having a routine. (If I had a routine, I wouldn't be able to work off adrenaline!)

When it comes to hobbies, sports, and other leisurely activities or just getting out of bed in the morning, we all need and enjoy a certain amount of adrenaline. However, like too much of anything, it can become addictive and unhealthy. Follow the strategies I have shared with you here, and you will be well on your way to breaking free of adrenaline's addictive chains.

Go Do: Take the Adrenaline Assessment

Take time to answer the adrenaline assessment above right now. Total your score of the statements that resonated with you.

Then schedule a recurring time in your routine to return to them throughout the year to assess your progress with kicking your adrenaline habit and tapping more into momentum and becoming a process-minded thinker.

[PART THREE]

SELF-ACCOUNTABILITY

CHAPTER 21

How to Manage Expected Interruptions

How to Protect Your Time

I nterruptions are part of our days. Whether they take the form of an impromptu meeting, a client-service problem, a last-minute proposal, personal demands, e-mails, or conversations with your staff, these unplanned engagements or activities have a tendency to rob us of time throughout our days, regardless of how intentional we are around scheduling our time.

While the majority of these distractions that inadvertently consume our day can be eliminated, the fact remains, many cannot. However, do not despair, there is hope—if you can't eliminate them, you can learn how to manage them better.

Robert, the owner of a media company, called me the other day, sharing his frustration about not being able to get through his daily list of responsibilities due to the constant barrage of interruptions from both customers and his staff.

Not wanting to be the "bad guy" or send the wrong message to his staff that he doesn't care, Robert allowed his employees to interrupt him with their questions, problems, and requests for help. Whether it was via e-mail, phone, a text, or them walking into his office and taking a seat in front of his desk, Robert had a tendency to drop what he was doing in fear of any additional fallout or backlash if he did not address their needs immediately.

To quell this ongoing problem, I shared a process with Robert to do a better job of managing the interruptions and the expectations people have of him. This way, he can be the one to take ownership of his time and his day rather than allowing the daily chaos, interruptions and distractions to dominate him.

Although a component of his solution was tactical ("Planning for the Unplanned," chapter 13), it's important to recognize that the solution to Robert's problem had less to do with a tactical solution to better manage his day, and more to do with a communication strategy that would protect his time without the collateral damage that often ensues.

Here's an example of a two-step communication process you can leverage the next time one of your employees comes to you with a pressing issue. And the best part is, you get to protect your time, coach the other person on time management and prioritization, and manage that interruption without being the bad guy.

Step One: Acknowledge and Confirm Urgency

You're sitting at your desk. The phone rings or someone walks into your office asking you, "Do you have a few minutes?" Rather than respond with the yes that's going to quickly become a trigger point of contention for you, first manage your visceral reaction to say yes. Instead, respond by saying, "Cathy, I'm in the middle of completing something right now that has a measurable deadline around it. However, I want to be as supportive and responsive as I can to your request. I want to ensure that whatever you need, I give it the time and the attention it deserves so that we can successfully work through it together. While I know it's important to you that we handle this now, is this something that demands immediate attention and must be handled right away, or can it wait until a little later, when I can better focus my time and attention on this?"

Let's face it. Everyone who asks for help thinks that what they're working on is the single most important thing of the day. They think it needs to be handled immediately when, in most cases, people create self-imposed pressure by reacting rather than thinking it through to respond in a healthier way. This also becomes a powerful coaching moment for the person you're speaking with.

While we all want the help people at the time they ask for it, the majority of issues may not be all that time-sensitive, even though everything today is positioned as an immediate priority. Everything is important to the person who is requesting your assistance; the response I suggested acknowledges rather than dismisses their request. And in some cases, it may not be something that can wait! But that's okay.

After all, if we can cut down on these types of distractions by 50 percent, that's more than 50 percent ownership that you just took back over your day to own it.

Regardless, while you are being sensitive to how people are feeling, some things can actually wait. The difference is, you're making them feel really good about waiting! However, if you never ask, you never create the opportunity to distinguish between what's urgent and what is not.

Step Two: Demonstrate Respect, Coach, and Schedule

Once they tell you how pressing their matter is, you now have the choice to assess the situation and either handle it in the immediate moment or find the time to address it at a later time. You'll find that many of these urgent requests can be postponed because they are not truly emergencies. Once you uncover that the situation is not as pressing as initially presented, continue with the following response:

"Okay, then, how about you and I discuss this (suggest a time that works for you) tomorrow morning at ten o'clock, when I know I can give this the time it needs, work through this together without feeling pressured or rushed, and give you my undivided attention without being distracted. Does that work for you?"

Who's not going to want their boss's undivided attention? Notice what you're not doing here. You're not telling them, "I'll be done in five minutes. Let's talk then." The fact is, most of the time, whatever it is you are currently engaged in, you won't be done in five minutes. This allows you to become more realistic with what you have on your plate.

So look at your schedule. Then plan this conversation for a time when you know will not be fiercely competing with other tasks you need to handle that command your attention.

Taking this approach removes the risk of coming across as self-righteous, uncaring, and insensitive when you say, "I can't help you now" or "You know what to do here, so just do it" or "How long have you been in this position"?" or "I'm too busy now; I'll try to find some time later to help you."

Now you can address the person's request in a respectful, supportive way while honoring the boundaries you are setting to protect yourself and your time from other people's continued barrage of demands. Rather than compete with distractions or feel as if you're helpless to do anything about them, simply learn to manage them and the expectations people have of you simply by communicating more effectively.

CHAPTER 22

Empower Your Calendar to Hold You Accountable

Beware of the Accountability Trap

T he accountability trap is yet another diversionary tactic. I had a client who owned a profitable business and was looking to take his company to the next level of success. At the end of our meetings, we would discuss the measurable tasks he would like to complete by our next meeting.

I noticed, however, that at the end of our meetings, he never took the time to write down the tasks he committed to finishing. So when we met the following week for our coaching session, I would ask him about the work he said he would complete. He responded by saying, "Oh, I completely forgot!"

I gave him the benefit of the doubt the first time, even the second time this occurred. During our third meeting, the writing was on the wall. His diversionary tactic had been exposed! Because he didn't write things down, he didn't remember what he said he would commit to doing. And because he didn't remember it, he didn't have to be accountable for it!

Consider for a moment that the absence of a routine frees you from being accountable for doing certain things you may not want to do but have to do to reach your goals (coaching/supporting your staff, prospecting, planning, finding a better career opportunity, getting in better physical shape, building your personal brand, vying for that promotion, cold calling, reporting, etc.).

Here's another diversionary tactic: "I'm so busy that I don't have the time to create my routine!"

Empower your routine to hold you accountable for doing the things you need to do to create the results and the lifestyle you want. One can argue, especially as a business owner, that there's no one around you who can truly hold you accountable. You're the boss!

So your routine has to be where your day starts and where it ends. After all, life works a whole lot easier when you do what you say you are going to do.

Go Do: Identify Your Top Three Diversionary Tactics

We all have things on our plates that we just don't want to do. And we all employ the use of diversionary tactics to procrastinate doing them.

Following the questions below, you will be better prepared to recognize and handle them the next time they creep into your work.

1. Write down your top three diversionary tactics, and put them in writing.

2. What do you tend to do instead of completing important tasks you're not interested or motivated to work on?

3. How do you avoid doing the work that matters? Is there a story that justifies this behavior as well?

4. Ask yourself, "Am I making this worse than it really is? How long will it actually take me to complete this task that's been on my desk for a month?"

5. Ask yourself, "Will I choose to empower my routine to hold me accountable and instill or recognize the consequence of not doing so?

CHAPTER 23

Acknowledge Your Successes—
Now!

Take a Moment to Pat Yourself on the Back

It's critical to recognize how productive you are or how much you are actually accomplishing each day. Honoring an effective routine is the greatest activity for continued success because it is aligned with the activities that, compounded over time, will create the achievements and lifestyle you desire. Develop other measurements of success such as daily, weekly, and monthly milestones so that you can recognize your achievements along the way rather than relentlessly striving to achieve more with no end in sight. Turn your binoculars around so that you are magnifying what you are doing and minimizing what you aren't.

Here are a few things to know as you go through this process.

Your Routine Will Evolve

A client of mine told me that if he is unable to follow through on one thing he had planned for in his routine, he'd become frustrated and toss the rest of his routine out the window for the remainder of the day. Although he believed he was a good self-starter, he wasn't good at restarting. In his mind, his routine was either perfect and in sync or he would think it wasn't working, and he'd give up on the remainder of his schedule.

The fact is, even though one item on your routine may not go according to plan, the remainder of your routine may be effective and work great. I can assure you, as you enhance and strengthen your relationship with time and continue to refine your activities so they best support your goals, your routine will evolve as well.

Instead of thinking, "My routine is not working" or asking yourself "Why can't I follow this?" use a situation as an opportunity to learn how to better manage your time and make your routine even more effective. Ask yourself, "What can I learn from this? Am I overcommitting? What needs to change? Am I being realistic with my externalities and how long each task takes to complete?"

Be creative when developing solutions for managing yourself. If one strategy doesn't work for you, don't force it. Instead, see what you can do to modify it so that it's better aligned with your values, talents, and strengths.

Here's another thought: If you have a tendency to deviate from your routine once you encounter one component that's not working, consider the possibility that this may be one of your diversionary tactics. In other words, this actually gives you the right not to follow your routine!

Perfection Is Paralysis

There will be times when you will be able to honor your routine completely and times when you will not. Give yourself permission to go through some learning curves and make adjustments. If you can't honor your schedule perfectly, that's okay. Give yourself a break! All that may be needed is a simple revision of the timelines you have allocated for certain activities. However, if you are having trouble honoring your routine throughout the week, you may need to take a closer look and evaluate where the breakdown is. Being flexible and open to change will enable you to think clearly and uncover new solutions and opportunities that would otherwise go undetected.

Now is the time to own your day!

Go Do: Take a Moment to Pat Yourself on the Back

Congratulations! You made it. Go ahead and pat yourself on the back for making the time to invest in yourself so that you can finally unlock the secrets to owning your day. In the few hours it took for you to read this book, think about the hours you will save, along with the increase in productivity, sales, harmony, and value you will deliver by implementing what you've learned.

You have found what you need to take back your day. Now it's time to coach your direct reports, peers, cross-functional teams, boss, customers, and family to do the same. Enjoy the power and fulfillment that comes from *owning your day*!

Part Three—Summary

1. Prioritizing Doesn't Work

It's impossible to prioritize when everything is a priority. It's more about who is screaming the loudest or where your greatest ROI is as the result of completing a certain task.

2. Multitasking Is Evil

Stop trying to multitask. Choose to do just one thing at a time—and do it with precision, focus, and unconditional commitment.

3. Eliminate Your To-Do List

Retire your to-do list. Work everything that matters into your routine.

4. Stop Focusing on Results

The result is the process. Miracles happen when you pay attention to how you're going to achieve the result rather than continually focusing solely on the result.

5. Get Off the Adrenaline Train

Adrenaline seems to be the drug of choice for sales leaders. It's time to choose a healthier drug: momentum.

6. How to Manage Expected Interruptions

Respond in a way that sets the expectations in a conversation and its importance to the other person to create more structured time for you. This also will allow the other person to generate solutions without you.

7. Empower Your Calendar to Hold You Accountable

Choose to pay attention to your calendar, or there will be implications. Expose your diversionary tactics.

8. Acknowledge Your Successes—Now!

Take a moment to appreciate what you've accomplished so far! Allow the activity to be the reward, not just the result.